STRIKE PATTERNS

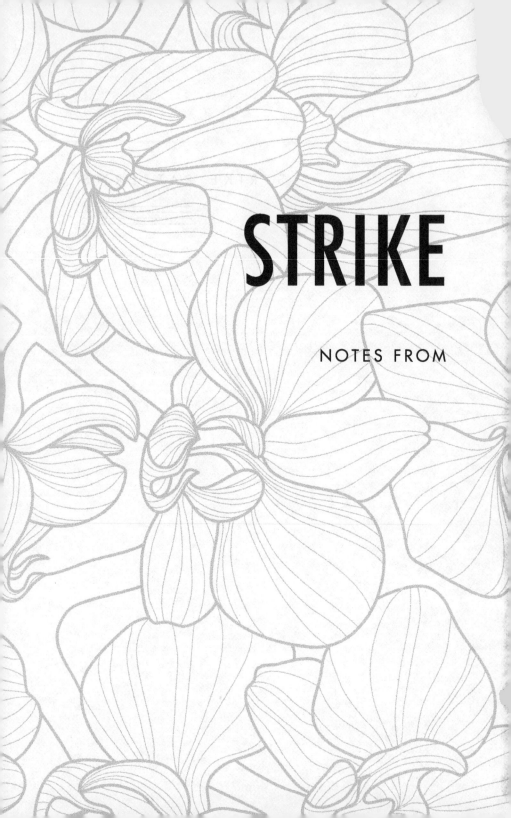

STRIKE

NOTES FROM

PATTERNS

POSTWAR LAOS

Leah Zani

REDWOOD PRESS | Stanford, California

REDWOOD PRESS

Stanford, California

Printed in the United States of America on acid-free, archival-quality paper

Library of Congress Cataloging-in-Publication Data

Names: Zani, Leah, 1986- author.

Title: Strike patterns : notes from postwar Laos / Leah Zani.

Description: Stanford, California : Redwood Press, 2022. |
    Includes bibliographical references.

Identifiers: LCCN 2021049996 (print) | LCCN 2021049997 (ebook) |
    ISBN 9781503611733 (cloth) | ISBN 9781503630710 (epub)

Subjects: LCSH: Vietnam War, 1961–1975—Campaigns—Laos—Fiction. |
    Vietnam War, 1961–1975—Aerial operations, American—Fiction. |
    Laos—History—1975—Fiction. | LCGFT: Nonfiction novels.

Classification: LCC PS3626.A6376 S77 2022 (print) | LCC PS3626.
    A6376 (ebook) | DDC 813/.6—dc23/eng/20211029

LC record available at https://lccn.loc.gov/2021049996

LC ebook record available at https://lccn.loc.gov/2021049997

Cover design: Kevin Barrett Kane

Cover Illustration: Adobe Stock

Text design: Kevin Barrett Kane & Rob Ehle

Typeset by Rob Ehle in 11/14 Arno Pro

Origins

During the periods that I studied in Laos between 2012 and 2015, I spent the longest span living in a village in Vientiane known for its religious devotion. This village radiated outward from a bright gilded wat (a Theravada Buddhist temple) itself built around the ruins of a much older shrine to a local female deity. The roads of this village were festooned with lilac jacaranda and other trees, more splendid still, most of whose names and colors I cannot identify but see clearly in my memory. Year round, I recall that petals drifted in confetti currents through the streets.

Pilgrims were regular visitors in my neighborhood: I watched them buying materials for prayers from vendors who set up shop in the shade of a particular species of flowering tree. Depending on whom I asked, the trees surrounding the wat were known either as cannonball trees—they had massive melon-sized fruits that were smooth and patinaed, like cannonballs; or Buddha trees—their flowers revealed miniature frilled thrones with a central pollinarium, floating like the Buddha on the back of the great naga that vowed to protect him from the forces of evil. The cannon and the divinity grew on the same tree.

Most pilgrims bought birds to carry their prayers. The little brown prayer birds appeared to be all of the same species: small, sexless, inconspicuous, with an unassuming urban twitter that lacked music. This blessed go-between of heaven and earth had a small, sharp black beak for picking insects out of the air. Each had eyes that were jet black and purely opaque. When a pilgrim purchased a prayer bird, the bird came in a bamboo cage only a few inches high and too small for the creature to release its wings. One wall of the cage was loose and could be lifted.

A friend, the person who inspired Chantha's character in this novel, took me to the wat to release prayer birds. We bought our birds—two identical brown specimens—and walked into the large temple plaza shaded by cannonball trees. Following her instructions, I brought my bird up to my mouth, still in its cage, and whispered my prayers into its hidden ears:

"I ask for wisdom in my research. I ask for clarity to understand what is important in my data, and for the safety of myself and everyone who participates in my study."

Unsure of which deities would be receptive to an unbeliever, I asked my bird to carry my prayer to the deity or spirit most suited to fulfill it. I do not know what my friend prayed for.

When I pulled up the loose wall of the cage, our two birds swooped skyward in twin arcs that crossed each other in the blue sky. I tried to follow their flight, but quickly lost track of my particular bird in the dense air traffic above the temple. So many birds, how could I choose only one to follow?

Later, I heard from a neighbor that the local vendors got their birds back by catching them in traps outside the temple walls: catch-and-release prayers. Our birds never got far enough to deliver their messages.

I remember also a prayer bird left in its cage on the steps of the wat. A few inches away, a scrawny black cat sat expectantly watching the stuck bird, paws neatly tucked underneath its nimble bulk as if pretending patience. The vendors were not the only ones setting traps for prayers.

What do I do with these frustrated hopes? Prayers, caught or killed before delivery? Where should I deliver my messages so that they will be received? Might there be a language, perhaps a genre of storytelling, best suited to share these fraught experiences of incompleteness—a way to trace the paths stories leave across the sky, like the cloudtrails of airplanes—a language to express what it feels like to live in a place massively impacted by decades of warfare and military waste?

This book is the result of many years of careful thinking about how best to research and write about war. I am a cultural anthropologist of war. Cultural anthropology is the study of human practices and the ways we give our lives meaning. Using qualitative and field-based methods, I investigate the social and cultural systems that produce violence and repair. After much thought and practice, I have come to believe that creative and literary methods are essential to holistically conveying the complexities of my research in ways that compel ethical action.

In *Strike Patterns*, I combined the qualitative tools of ethnography with the empathetic registers of literature to nurture the open-ended, compassionate investigation that is vital to sustaining peaceful societies. I wrote *Strike Patterns* to invite you into that space of shared inquiry, action, and emotional responsiveness to warfare and military waste. These stories are invitations to pay attention and be present for how people live in these Lao battlefields, which are also American battlefields. When I share these stories, I am inviting you to pay attention and participate in the creative labor that is postwar life: an American postwar life as well as a Lao postwar life, though Laos has been hurt by the greater burden of America's violent indifference, and the domestic effects of American imperialism are suffered most by people of color and not the white elite.

The stories in *Strike Patterns* are not tidy narratives with clear ends and clean hands. Literary methods are powerful because they mimic the necessary creative labor of living alongside war, racism, structural violence, and all the other large and small atrocities of our daily lives. We make our lives out of this mess, we tell ourselves stories, and our lives are meaningful.

A Lao bomb technician once asked me, "Where is the safe land?" and I had no answer, for I see how American imperialism has turned everywhere into a battlefield. As an anthropologist, I am drawn to study cluster bombing because this style of warfare specifically targets social infrastructures and cultural systems. The goal of the Laos model of warfare was to break down an existing society and replace it with a more politically amenable society. Everyday life is the battlefield, targeted from above. Violence does transform society—but rarely in a predictable way, and certainly not as a means of creating a viable, functioning alternative. I hear this technician's question as a necessary provocation for peace: Where do we feel safe? And how do we get from here to that place of shared safety? As of this writing, the United States (along with China, Russia, Israel, India, Pakistan, and Brazil) has yet to sign the Convention on Cluster Munitions and is still actively selling and using these dangerously indiscriminate weapons. And Laos, for its part, has yet to sign the Landmine Ban and is stockpiling antipersonnel weapons, presumably for use against its own population.

I began writing poetry and fiction as a way to write against terror, both the lingering terror of America's war and the present terror of the Lao authoritarian state. Past war violence layers beneath the current violence of the state, including suppression of civil society, police harassment, surveillance, secret detention camps, and extrajudicial killings. I am writing about Laos, but I might also be describing race violence in the United States: as I write this in July 2020, streets in my Oakland neighborhood and many neighborhoods across America are ablaze with Black Lives Matter protests and federal reprisals that include police harassment, surveillance, arrests, and detention centers.

These are two systems of state terror separated by differences of degree, not type. The Lao state inherited a system of colonial and imperial violence, and today is among the world's most repressive regimes. Accounts of state terror riddled my interviews and field visits, contributing to a collective fear and silence. My friends regularly reminded me that it was unsafe to openly talk about the state. This final repression deprived people of the power to share their own stories. Before I left Laos, a colleague there warned me that "connecting the dots is very political. If you want to keep working in this country after you publish, you have to be very careful about what you write."

When I was writing my first book, the academic monograph *Bomb Children*, I knew that it was important to write against this silence, but I couldn't figure out how to "connect the dots" without potentially harming myself or my research subjects. *Bomb Children* contained no names, few personal details, and no portraits of people except for Sombath Somphone, a man disappeared by the Lao police during my fieldwork and presumed murdered. It was too risky for me to reveal the living, breathing persons and events of my research. I felt frustrated that I could not share some of my best and most tender stories.

My first book vexed me with thorny, perennial issues of disclosure, public impact, and political relevance: How can I best protect my research subjects? What knowledge should be shared, and what withheld? Just to know something isn't enough, but how to make something known in a way that changes who we are? What kind of knowledge is actionable for social good? There was still so much left that I wanted to write, and I wanted to write for a wider audience and greater public impact.

Responding to these questions, I wrote *Strike Patterns* as ethnographic fiction. Ethnography is both a method and a genre; it describes a way of researching and writing about the world based on in-depth field studies of everyday life. Ethnography is characterized by holism, respect for human diversity, and caring attention to context and detail. Building on this discipline, ethnographic fiction is a hybrid genre for writing research-based creative stories. The genre doesn't neatly fit into fiction or nonfiction, but instead occupies a fertile gray area that (at its best) encourages open-ended thinking about what is possible rather than what is real. I think that anthropologists are drawn to literary methods because we want to participate in the creative labor of making culture. Fiction gives us access to cultural and emotional registers that are often suppressed in academic writing, though these are of intrinsic value to the topics and people we study. Fiction makes ethnography, and ethnographers, more human in our striving toward better worlds.

Ethnographers are writers as much as researchers. Clifford Geertz, a prominent anthropologist and popular author of the last century, called ethnography a genre of faction, combining elements of fact and fiction. The most common fictions in ethnography are forms of subject protections: pseudonyms, composite characters, and composite places. We use fiction to protect our research subjects and ourselves. Meditating further on Geertz's ideas and an essay on the same theme by Carole McGranahan, I believe that ethnographers *make stuff* without *making stuff up,* and this labor to make stuff sets our writing apart from journalists' accounts. What are we making? We are most often making social theories, concepts, and models of social life and interpersonal relations that enable people to do work in the world; and sometimes we are also creating models of more equitable social systems, even entirely different worlds or universes.

Anthropologists often write fiction: Gabriel Tarde's strange Victorian sci-fi vision *Underground Man;* Claude Lévi-Strauss' account of colonial decay in Brazil, *Tristes Tropiques,* which is more often read as a novel than as an ethnography; Zora Neale Hurston's body of transformative, moving work about Black America, including *Mules and Men* and *Their Eyes Were Watching God;* Bruno Latour's *Aramis,* a hybrid novel that he describes as scientifiction; Ursula Le Guin's *The Left Hand of Darkness* that puts galactic ethnographers on other planets entirely; and, more recently, the creative ethnographic prose of Amitav Ghosh, Hugh Raffles, and Kathleen Stewart, among many others. Writing for a broader audience, these authors are intentionally participating in public culture rather than merely documenting it for scholars.

In its messiness and ambiguity, fiction offers a respectful representation of the ways that people experience ghosts and the other phantasmagoria of everyday life. When writing about communities like Chantha's, I chose to write fiction to accurately convey the complexities of real life—and sometimes, real life is unreal, beyond belief. I did not make up the ghosts of these villages (they were real to my research subjects), and I chose to write them as real. Anthropologists are less interested in what is or isn't real and more interested in the implications of different beliefs about what is real. In terms of reader impact, there is a huge difference between writing about war ghosts as real and writing about war ghosts as local belief. At its worst, the latter is dismissive and infantilizing, reinforcing colonial hierarchies by provincializing local beliefs in relation to an assumed superior, more rational culture. We must feel our way beyond these hierarchies if we are to create a more peaceful world. I take responsibility for these representational choices because I believe we have passed the point of merely informing or explaining this violence and must instead work toward a more accessible and responsive engagement that acknowledges our common human needs.

The United States covertly bombed Laos from 1964 to at least 1973 and in violation of the 1962 Geneva Accords declaring Laos neutral territory. The Secret War was a testing ground for a new means of war, including some of the first uses of computer-directed bombing, antipersonnel bombs, aerial gunships, modern cluster bombing, and drone warfare. This conflict also inaugurated the global presence of the paramilitary Central Intelligence Agency (CIA) and was a critical laboratory for modern techniques of covert and counterinsurgency warfare. The Laos model of warfare has become the template for war in our modern era, including a now familiar combination of massive aerial bombardment, minimal ground troops, large civilian casualties, covert paramilitary involvement, and highly politicized humanitarian assistance.

The scale of the Lao conflict was unprecedented: the United States dropped more than two million tons of ordnance on Laos, all on a country the size of Utah. An amount equivalent to one ton of ordnance per person. Imagine, one ton of bombs marked to kill you, and a ton each for the members of your family and your neighbors. In total, roughly 200,000 people died during the Secret War—about one in ten. And more than a quarter of Laos' population fled as war refugees, many of them settling in the American Midwest and California's Central Valley. Parts of Laos were abandoned, whole cities depopulated and destroyed, forests defoliated and now growing back as tender saplings. Since the war ended forty years ago, these bombs have caused at least 20,000 additional casualties. Laos remains one of the most massively war-contaminated countries in the world. "Massive" is a technical term in the international clearance sector describing contamination over more than 1,000 square kilometers. Bomb technicians created the category of massive contamination specifically to describe the American cluster bombing of Vietnam and Laos. Hidden in plain sight, this carnage makes the secrecy of the war more shocking.

The Secret War remains secret. Laos was never officially at war, and there has been no sustained public reckoning in either Laos or America—I write fiction as a comment on this blatant obfuscation in the face of widespread, ongoing violence. Collectively, on both sides of this old conflict, we have been denied the ability to regret, grieve, forgive, or process our own warfare. As I write this, President Trump is deporting many Lao refugees back to Laos, where they will almost certainly be targeted as enemies of the communist state. Many were supporters of the Secret War who sought refuge in the United States, their supposed ally, and have now lived here for forty years. To send them back to Laos is to deny the war and its ongoing impact. Such policies tell stories of American nationalism that justify or erase imperial violence. *Pay attention.* Readers and reviewers for this book sometimes asked me, "But what is real?" This is exactly the question I want readers to investigate and that I refuse to clarify. My hope is that readers will question how their own experiences of reality—what is real, what is over, what is accidental, what is American, what is violence, what is war, what is peace—have been shaped by political agendas and social histories.

At every public talk or reading of my work, I am approached afterward by a person my age or younger, the child of war refugees, soldiers, humanitarian workers, or peace protesters from the

Vietnam-American War. Their concerns are familiar to me: often, I see the shock of recognizing the imprint of violence in our lives, a kind of hidden wound that marked our parents and therefore our childhoods but remained unexamined until we were adults. I imagine that, like me, their desires to understand led them to explore their familial and social histories.

War is always passed down from one generation to the next, and America's forever wars are causing specific intergenerational wounds: in America and Laos, we are living without justice and without peace, under threat of neverending violence. Sometimes, awareness of violence is the missing context that we need to understand our own lives, our parents' fears, our childhood games, our anxieties and vulnerabilities. This is my generation: we have grown up in relation to our parents' wars and have inherited a social burden from our parents that we must now learn how to put to rest. This novel is my effort to remedy this social burden and exorcise these ghosts of war.

After more than ten years as a practicing academic, I no longer believe that it is possible to get to that space of shared, multigenerational inquiry via conventional scholarship alone. I am keenly aware that social theory, in and of itself, is not enough to make something meaningful to a reader. That takes a story—whether fiction, nonfiction, or ethnography, it must be a story. My poems and creative nonfiction are published in popular magazines that would never publish my academic articles. Scholarship presents arguments to convince experts, and the ethical action of scholarship is inherently prescriptive and exclusionary; in comparison, stories may be more invitational, and their ethical action is participatory and open-ended. We change culture by living it, and this is precisely how stories make sense.

At the temple in my old neighborhood, birds in flight traced our prayers through the sky, but each bird kept a private prayer for its own safe landing. Every message fell back to earth, to us.

Oakland, California
July 3, 2020

STRIKE PATTERNS

1

CHANTHA TOLD ME A STORY, a well-worn story that I had heard before, and that she picked up like a pebble and worried in her pocket:

A group of three brothers found a wrecked plane in the jungle, lost during the Secret War and abandoned by its pilots. Now their secret. The brothers dismantled the plane and carried each piece, by foot, to their village to use for barter and sale on the local scrap market. Two of the brothers used machetes to cut down bamboo growing near the crash site and built a shoulder gurney; the third wove a carrying basket with one long strap across his forehead. And so the plane began to disintegrate, every metal tube and aluminum sheet in the wings carefully cut and carried away. To make it easier to transport the remainder, they set a massive fire under the fuselage. The light aluminum melted into large, dull puddles that cooled hard and could be easily collected. The fire became a cold cloud of ash, floating in the air, stirred by their fingers, like fish scales shimmering underwater. And beneath the ash, the tarred engine sunk still deeper into the black soil as if dropped again from a great height. Too heavy to carry—the brothers left the engine in the jungle.

It was the most significant war scrap sale in memory—more money than could be made farming rice.

As it was, it was still an old military plane, and its bolts rattled, the engine so loud that the whole cabin groaned, my hand vibrating where I touched the hull. I looked around as I took my seat but noticed no evidence of its wartime history. The plane had been hollowed out and scraped clean like a split passionfruit. Every surface, including the floor, was coated in thick layers of high-gloss white paint. Cabin air was flat and wet, and there was a lingering smell of human sweat, too fresh, emanating from the permanently damp upholstery of the chairs. What had this plane carried during the war, before diplomats, business scouts, aid workers, and backpackers? The added seats, scavenged from some other aircraft, were lightly bolted to the floor such that they shifted, creaking, in turbulence.

Looking out the tiny cabin window, I watched the landscape expand in detail beneath me as we descended: patchwork rectangles of rice paddies, dyed in shades from neon green to dull ochre; square corrugated roofs; the pale lines of roads and footpaths, even a single, straight paved road that terminated at the airport ahead. My seat creaked as I leaned forward to watch parcels of farmland emerge from the jungle, bright green beneath me and pale, nearly gray, in the distance. The landscape drifted in gray dust at the horizon like a disintegrating remembrance. As the airplane flew lower, the fields and farms below rose from my memory:

I saw myself two weeks ago, walking in a field at dusk, and Chantha walking beside me. She was talking about her decision to leave her village and attend university in the capital city several days' journey upriver. "There are no opportunities in the village: everyone must leave, if we want to live a better life," she explained. On either side of our dirt path, the low sun lit the tips of the new rice shoots bright yellow, glowing. I caught the lead line of her family's water buffalo and walked toward the docile animal. Shepherding the family's buffalo; this had been Chantha's chore before she entered the finance program at university. Shoulder-deep in a round mud pond, the animal looked up at me with long-lashed, large eyes slowly blinking. The mud pond was precisely the length of a buffalo's body from nose to tail and precisely the depth of a buffalo's shoulder. I untangled the lead line from the reeds by the pond, where the tarred rope had caught. The animal slowly lifted itself out of the mud, one glistening hoof at a time. "Maa," *come* in Lao, Chantha said once, sweetly. I didn't have to pull on the lead line; she knew it was time to go home.

I saw that field out the plane's cabin window—but now seen from above. The blue tiles on the roof of Chantha's house. Her family rice fields, now a fading yellow. The white rectangle of the wat. The communist party office and its ornament of tattered red flags. A line of motorbikes parked outside the office. The garbage pile, blackened, invisible under a smudge of smoke. The buffalo pond. From this height, I could see the ponds arranged in an elliptical pattern: part of a cluster munition strike? Circular clustered ponds reflecting the clouds as bright flashes of white. The more I looked, the more certain I was that they were bomb craters, not only ponds. Past the fields, the cavities had been filled in with dirt, partially obscured by houses built on top of them. Fifty years after the secret bombing of Laos during the Vietnam-American War and the footprint of this airstrike was still clearly visible from above. By its longest edge, the pattern of craters was longer than the village itself.

Separated by the floating clouds, the war that I saw from the old airplane was a parallel world, present but hard to recognize in life below. The plane was flying low enough that I distinguished a herd of buffalo lumbering across the village road, their haunches painted pale with drying mud. The shepherd was nowhere visible with this herd. We were flying at the height of a bomber. And from that height, and in this old military plane, I briefly imagined myself an American pilot in the Secret War in the 1960s and 70s, dropping my load of cluster munitions to create the strike pattern I now traced below.

I easily imagined this view from the air: I come from a family of pilots all the way back to the first wooden biplanes. My dad, Christine, flew a plane—she learned from her father, who had been a wingwalker and a barnstormer in a flying circus, and then later a notable engineer for Pan Am. My dad's gender transition removed her from the male line of family pilots; by the time I was born, she no longer had a pilot's license, and there was a protective distance between herself and her dad. I knew about my grandfather's red Curtiss Robin, a three-seater monoplane of the early twentieth century, without knowing much else about him. Christine did not hang any photos of him in our home, but she did display a photo of granddad's China Clipper slipping into a water landing on the San Francisco Bay. Our house was decorated with travel trophies of family aviation: carved ivory, foreign cookware, wooden masks and statuettes, black pearls, an ostrich egg, and even an entire leopard skin. Two of my great uncles had been Air Force pilots. I grew up hearing stories of corkscrew dives, pilots flipping bombs on the tips of their wings, ships destroyed in conflagrations seen from above, blind night runs over the Pacific, the invention of radar, ditched landings, and daring rescues from tropical islands. These were children's stories without suffering or people, empty as toy planes. As an adult, I hear something naïve in these stories. Their bloodlessness betrays the pilot's privilege of distance, the privilege of watching violence from the air.

Every air war has its *strike pattern*, a signature of violence that is best seen from above in the shape of the wreckage. When I was doing fieldwork in Laos with explosives clearance teams, I learned that strike pattern is a technical term that describes the patterns of craters, ordnance, debris, and other material evidence leftover from aerial warfare and weapons. Clearance technicians use strike patterns to identify airstrikes and predict the size and scope of their clearance projects. To do this, a technician might use satellite imagery, even hand-drawn maps, to gain an aerial perspective—like my view out the airplane window.

And yet, the social and cultural consequences of the Secret War far exceed this pattern of physical destruction. Surrounding each crater is a much larger impact zone of loss, safety, fear, stigma, and hope. This much larger sociocultural strike pattern cannot be seen from above but must be felt in the intricate details of daily life. Culture is lived from the ground up. To fully map the strike patterns of this air war, I learned to see from the ground as easily as from the air.

Planes flew over Chantha's home every afternoon. Her small village was beneath the flight path from the capital city to the provincial airport—the path I would later trace in that old military plane. The planes flew low, already beginning their descent over Chantha's blue-tiled roof. The deep grumble of their engines approached rapidly and then receded into the hush of the rustling rice fields.

Mali, Chantha's young niece, stretched her chubby hand up to follow the airplane overhead. Her small, dark eyes watched, curious. She was wearing purple galoshes decorated with yellow flowers, already muddy, plus matching little yellow flowers on each of her two tiny ponytails.

"Ganom, ganom," Chantha said. *My sweet, my sweet.* She was holding Mali gently on the seat of her crossed legs. We sat on the terrace of an old farmhouse maintained as a recreational river lookout. Chantha's home village was made up of less than a dozen stilt houses rising above the wet fields. It was the end of the rains season, and the cinnamon-colored river was flooding, its peak only a few feet below the farmhouse terrace. A low railing, each wooden slat carved with one immortal champa flower, separated us from the Mekong River.

"Mali talks, but not in front of strangers." Chantha smiled at me, switching to English to proudly explain her niece's behavior. "She loves seeing airplanes cross over the village every day as they fly to the airport. My hope is that one day, Mali will leave and become an airplane pilot."

She bounced her niece on her legs and repeated in Lao: "Ganom, would you like to learn to fly?" The child laughed, and then, capricious, fidgeted off Chantha's lap and began vigorously exploring the terrace.

Chantha was the first person in her village to attend university in Vientiane, where she had been living since graduating with a degree in finance. Her transition to the capital had been difficult; she had few city connections to help her create her new life. But her English was excellent, and she was quick to get a job as a finance officer for an explosives clearance operator headquartered in the capital. That was where I met Chantha. I came to Laos to do fieldwork for my anthropology Ph.D. program at a university in California. I was partnering with Chantha's employer, the clearance operator, for a study of postwar reconstruction. It was within our lifetimes that Laos' borders had opened to allow foreigners into the country. This new openness was what had brought both of us to work in the capital, by our different paths. She and I were the same age, building friendships in an unfamiliar city, learning a new language, and I felt this slim familiarity draw us to each other.

Chantha was not her real name. It was her playname—as is common in Laos, she had a public name that she gave to friends and colleagues. Chantha means moon; playnames are traditionally based on the person's unflattering characteristics, but I didn't know what characteristic of hers was moon-like. When I thought of Chantha as a moon, I thought of her strength exerting its own forceful pull. The other office staff at the clearance operator joked about Chantha being small: Was this what they meant by moon, small as the moon in the sky? On one occasion, she brought a bowl of tiny, tiny shrimp to a potluck, and kong noi, *small shrimp*, became another affectionate nickname. At her full height, Chantha came up barely to my shoulder. I never used that name. When I once read her real, private, legal name on an office report, I had to ask her who it was: "Myself, but only with my mother," she said.

As our friendship developed, Chantha invited me to join her on festival days at her neighborhood wat in Vientiane. I never had the gumption to attend on my own; I maintained a respectful distance from the wat unless invited, and I was secretly thrilled to be invited. Chantha taught me the meaning of Lao blessings—*may all bad things flow out and all good things flow in*—and that most rituals were in Pali, an ancient language of sacred texts that few understood. I learned how to tie a ritual scarf across my chest, pinned at the shoulder to stay in place. I mimicked Chantha's delicate bowing, pressing my forehead into the diamond shaped by my flexed fingers on the ground. After one of these visits, as we walked back to our bikes together, Chantha asked if I wanted to join her for a festival in her home village.

"We can travel together and stay with my mother and aunt," she said. "I want to show you my ban." She spoke the word ban, for *Lao village*, like a birthright or an inheritance. "You could see our Fireboat Festival; it is very beautiful and very important and maybe good for your cultural study."

This was the first time she'd invited me to travel with her out of the city.

I smiled sidelong, uncertain. "Do you mean it? You probably just don't want to travel by yourself."

"Of course, it's not good traveling by yourself!" Then she clasped my arm and shook me a little in warning, very gently. "Also, I am worried about you: you don't want to be a woman in the city for the festival by yourself, either." She crossed her hands in front of her as if to ward off misfortune. "It gets really crazy and crowded. Too much drinking! It will be safer in my ban."

She was certainly right: I had never stayed in the city during a major festival and would feel safer with a friend. Her comment made me feel like an awkward academic, intelligent but bad at parties, which wasn't too far off. I said yes.

From the farmhouse terrace, I looked over to the dark green banks of Thailand, visible but distant on the other side of the Mekong. On a clear day like this I felt that I could look downstream the full length of Thailand, all the way to the coast of Cambodia.

There was no homesickness for me in this landscape—nothing reminded me of dry California. The trees and colors were too wet and saturated. This land was smooth and regular, as if patted down by many hands, and had the quality of being regularly wiped clean by floods. Further inland, the rain scoured the sandstone karst into sharp cliffs. The cliffs shot up to shocking heights, outcrops of jungle suspended acres up. Cloud catchers wreathed in mist. Eventually, the cliffs merged to form the Annamite Mountain Range, a branch of the Himalayas whose spine kept Laos' northeastern border. The other border was the river. The country was one-half of a river valley, one-half of a long cloud chamber, a rain vessel. Blue-bruised rainclouds formed at the mountains or the ocean, where the high airs met, and blew into Laos like foreign airliners. Along the river routes, land was worn away by flows downslope from the mountains to the Mekong whose banks seasonally expanded with silt. Even Laos' dry season was damp—compared to the golden fields of California's fire season. Laos was too wet to feel familiar.

Across the river, the houses had electricity and, at night, shown like a line of candles floating on the water. By day, young men and women in long, narrow boats plied the swollen currents to cross the border. There were very few young adults, especially young men, on the Lao side of the river; all the young crossed over to work in Thailand or moved upstream to the capital. The Mekong and its tributaries tied the villages to each other by fast, liquid routes. If Chantha steered a motorboat upstream, it would eventually bring her to the capital.

Mostly, only the women came back.

In Chantha's village, women tied families to the land while men moved from place to place. Property and titles were inherited through the female line, mothers to daughters. Parents preferred daughters because they kept the property within the family line. Women were often in charge of property and finances; if a woman married, it was expected that her husband would leave his home village to live in hers. It was thought that women were naturally better at math than men and better suited to finance. All the finance staff at Chantha's office were women. What are men good at? I had asked, and she had rolled her eyes, "Drinking."

Mali wandered down to the riverbank, wearing her purple galoshes, and poked the water with a long piece of bamboo. The new grass on the bank was a vital neon green, nurtured by the fertile mud. Everything was so fresh that even the mud didn't smell yet. A string of bubbles popped the surface a little way out from the shore; there was something under the water.

Below the terrace, the surface of the water was wrinkled like skin, oily and slick, over a massive coiling thing unimaginably vast. This vast thing opened its mouth and lapped the riverbank, laved the undersides of the boats, gently rocked them between its teeth, and swallowed the wooden poles where the boats were tied. There were boulders in its gullet, steadily rolling down the throat of the river dragon. These were the dragons whose slithering bellies carved the rivers of Laos. The village had no river docks; the wooden piers would have been eaten whole each monsoon. Anything inserted into the water disappeared below the surface, sooner or later.

"That is where the river dragon lives, Mali! Don't play there, or he will eat you!"

The child looked up at us and giggled, showing us her mud-painted palms.

"Sabaidee!" From below, women's calls of Hello!

Chantha's mother, Mae, and aunt, Silavong, came walking down the path through the bamboo grove that separated the rice fields from the village proper. Tall plumes of bamboo feathered, waving mildly beyond the houses.

Silavong fetched her daughter from the water's edge. "Be careful, little one!"

Mae had a large blue plastic bucket balanced on one hip and held a hand-forged, blackened machete. She called up to us, an invitation: "We are just about to cut banana leaves for the fireboats."

The Fireboat Festival was an auspicious time of returns—and Chantha, like many, had returned home to honor it. Home villages were the lodestone of family and culture and the center of religious rituals like the Fireboat Festival. Watching the three generations of family women gather for the festival, I wondered: If Mali became an airplane pilot, would she remember to fly home?

Mae explained that there was a stand of banana trees near Old Uncle's house that the villagers hadn't picked in a while. The leaves were greener and broader. Each was longer than my arm, a dark yellow-green, with paler undersides frosted nearly white. A hundred closely spaced veins divided the leaves into parallel sections; they split quickly into even strips. The leaves rippled like raw silk in the breeze, frayed edges, little wisps of loose thread.

Mae deftly cut the greenest leaves with her machete.

Old Uncle watched us with friendly, silent interest while smoking a tarred hand-rolled cigarette. Almost toothless. He wore an old, tattered but recognizable military uniform with only one sleeve. No insignia; I noticed the outline of a missing designation patch torn from his remaining sleeve. By his age, I assumed that he fought in the war but had no clue as to which side. Old Uncle's house was a small lofted room reached by a ladder, attached to a large dirt patio under a thatched trellis for shade. The banana trees were his green walls on all four sides. On his shaded patio, water was boiling in a tin pot over a ceramic charcoal stove. There was a little pile of loose-leaf dried tea on a wooden divan next to the stove, a gift from Bua, a neighbor who gathered tea leaves from an abandoned colonial tea plantation in the forest. After decades of neglect, the tea had acquired a wild taste, rooted and robust. Mae left a few extra banana leaves next to his teapot to encourage Uncle to make his own little fireboat later.

I noticed Mae's thoughtful, silent encouragement. I wanted to be worthy of her hospitality—I was here on her invitation as much as

Chantha's—and I was trying to learn the village etiquette of small kindnesses. I reached over to pick up Mae's blue bucket now heavy with banana trunks and leaves, she acknowledging my gesture with a robust smile.

Ahead of me, the family talked about their day—even Mali, who must have decided that I was an okay stranger. I listened, a few steps behind, trying to follow their fast Lao conversation with my new language skills.

"Mali, my sweet, what did you eat today?"

"Old Uncle caught little fishes, and we fried them!"

When the adults spoke with each other, I had a harder time understanding their sentences, though I caught every few words: "Respected aunt, when do you think, Thailand, bus driver, candles, too young, temple." I had been studying the Lao language for nearly two years, but speaking Lao still felt like rolling marbles in my mouth: conversations often required a muscular strength and precision that I didn't have. The multiple tones and vowel lengths of Lao made it a laughing language of puns, sly winks, word play, rhymes, spells, and poetry.

By the road, we picked bright orange marigold flowers that were the color of Buddhist monks' robes. The women preferred to pick the plants that were already bent by the passage of motorbikes. I knew these flowers were edible, each dense inflorescence tightly packed with bitter orange petals. And also bright daisies, whose many thin scalloped rays surrounded a raised button. Silavong and Mali picked tiny jasmine buds from vines that grew along the field fence, delicate buds shaped like small cones of incense that had not yet opened to release their perfume.

"Why do monks wear orange?" I asked in Lao.

"The orange color reminds them of death." Chantha was holding a few spheres of marigold. I'd asked a child's question, and she'd had an answer ready. In the early stages of our research, anthropologists are like children learning a new culture with untrained senses. It can be a very awkward research method. Mali had probably asked the same question. "Orange is the color of dying leaves when the season changes. For this reason, this flower is used at a lot at festivals and funerals. Happy or sad, it reminds us that everything ends."

I nodded, a little embarrassed. I wanted to please her with my proper pronunciation. "And so we're using orange flowers at this festival?"

"Yes, we are making little boats to decorate with flowers and candles and incense." She wrinkled her brow as she considered how best to explain this to me. "But we aren't making the *real* fireboats—those can only be made by young people who aren't married. There are no more young unmarried people in our ban—they are all working in Thailand or the capital. So we are making a smaller kind of boat, simpler, out of banana leaves."

I thought about pointing out that Chantha was unmarried, but then I worried that I might accidentally be pointing out that she was too old. I had read that a full-sized fireboat was typically made by youths who timbered and hollowed a tree specially felled for the festival. The smaller, banana leaf boats were more commonly made by city dwellers who didn't have access to the tools or forest materials necessary for making full-sized boats.

"All of the boats are gifts for the water dragon that lives in our part of the river and protects us," Chantha went on. "It's supposed to be fun—we are trying to entertain the dragon and to make him laugh. And to ask his protection of any travelers on the river, especially friends and family who are working away from their ban."

"Protection for you and me? We work away from home."

"Ah, yes, like you and me." She hadn't initially thought to include me in her blessing for protection. An international traveler, with a frequent flyer card, maybe I didn't need the protection of the river dragon? "All kinds of travelers, not just people who travel on the river. The dragon can help with that—keep us safe."

Chantha's family house was a little walk down the road from the river overlook, further inland past Old Uncle's house. Once home, we four adults arranged our materials on the tiled floor: piles of banana leaves, heaps of different colored flowers, two pairs of scissors, sticks of candles and incense, and a machete. I peeked under my lashes at my hosts to make sure I had my materials correctly arranged.

There was no furniture but floor mats, floor cushions, a small woven round table-tray, and rolled bed mats (one of them mine) in the corner under the pink veils of mosquito net. Mint green walls and wood-shuttered windows. An old calendar, several years out of date, was the only wall decoration. The calendar showed a smiling young Lao woman in a beautifully tailored purple silk outfit holding a bouquet of white flowers. She fanned her perfectly shaped nails, also purple.

From the attached exterior kitchen out the rear door came the sour smell of fermenting baby onions with chilies—layered over the sweet, home-smell of day-old cooked sticky rice. There was a small refrigerator back there, the only one in the village, but rarely used. It was a gift from Chantha who bought it with her first year's city wages. Privately, Mae disapproved of the refrigerator: it chilled the food, which was unhealthful for naturally colder women, she said, and used up too much power from the generator.

In the far corner, a narrow ladder led to Mae's bedroom upstairs. Mae, as the highest status family member, slept in the uppermost bedroom; and above even her, up at the topmost spot where the roof beams joined together, was the family's shrine to the Buddha and local deities. Lao houses are small models of an ordered cosmos: trash in the understory beneath and gods in the rafters above. Somewhere in the middle, but a little bit closer to the garbage, I slept on a mat on the first floor.

I noticed that when Mae looked at her family, she often pressed her lips together tightly. Worry etched deep lines into her face, worn deeper by the sun. She had a stern, substantial presence that was also comforting, the heaviness of being in charge. Her hair she cut utilitarian short—rather than keeping it in a bun, as was typical of Lao matriarchs. She rarely smiled but had perfectly straight and white teeth that she treated with whitening strips from across the river. Mae was lucky to have so many sisters and daughters in the family. She inherited this house and these fields from her mother. Looking at her younger female relatives who all lived away from the village, she didn't know if any of them would live here after her.

When Silavong sat on a floor mat next to her, Mae carefully tucked a stray hair out of her younger sister's face.

"It is important that we make our boats carefully," Mae pronounced, patting an empty floor mat for me to sit on her other side. "Let me show you how we do it in our ban."

Mae had quick, dexterous hands and calloused fingers from hand-sewing. Her caramel skin was textured with small scars from farm labor. She ripped the banana leaves into strips, counting the veins of the leaves to measure even lengths. With the machete, she split the central stalk into many small spears—like wooden toothpicks. Fast as she was, she kept track of my work with side glances and was quick to correct my technique.

"Like this. Like I do it. If the lines are straight and the edges the same, it is better for your luck." She ran her finger along the seam of the banana leaf, showing me how the veins of the leaf were parallel to the right edge of each green triangle. Nodding, I carefully unfolded and corrected my triangles.

Once I had sufficient triangles, I used the toothpicks to pin them in a decorative pattern around the edge of a thin, circular slice of the banana tree trunk. The slab was spongy, nearly white, and very lightweight. The texture and color reminded me of styrofoam.

Chantha swirled the flowers in a bowl of water. Her hands were smooth, unblemished, softened, and bleached by hand creams. There were little pink spots of old nail lacquer on her fingernails. Next to her, Mali was babbling softly to herself, perplexed by the petals that stuck to her skin. Chantha handed me some of the clean flowers. "It is lucky to put colors on your boat," she said.

"Thank you."

"Ah, how beautiful! Very well done." That was Mae, inspecting my work. I had arranged the marigolds in two concentric rings within the boat. Following Mae's lead, I stuck two thin beeswax candles and two sticks of incense into the middle. Mae reached over and carefully inserted a single jasmine bud into the top point of an outer triangle—I completed the pattern, adding jasmine buds to each point.

"Do you know why we use green banana leaves?"

"No, but I'd like to hear that."

"Because green is the color of money." Not the color of Lao money, which comes in a range of pale pastels. Green is the color of American money. Orange and green; death and money.

When did I first learn about the war? It seems paradoxical to learn about a secret war: How does one reveal a secret that big, kept for half a century? It certainly cannot be done by a single person, all at once. In my memory, a precise date of revelation is as elusive as the historical details of the war. Another piece of grown-up history: at first, the war slipped unnoticed through my life. I have a hazy memory of Mr. Hart, my public high school social science teacher, mentioning Laos when telling our class about his anti–Vietnam War protests in Berkeley. I retain the memory of his moral outrage. Mr. Hart's spontaneous tirades about the failures of Vietnam were not on the syllabus—but it was his favorite subject, and he treated all other social science topics with perfunctory calm.

Mr. Hart mentioned bombings in Laos, saying "Lay-ows" the way that Kennedy pronounced it in 1961, though I did not learn this until I heard a recording of Kennedy's speech many years later: *I want to make it clear to the American people, and to all of the world, that all we want in Lay-ows is peace, not war—a truly neutral government, not a cold war pawn, a settlement concluded at the conference table and not on the battlefield.* Kennedy's pronunciation was as dubious as his policy; that year, the United States sent its first military forces to

Laos: soldiers disguised as civilians, flying unmarked bombers and helicopters. These Air America planes delivered weapons and supplies to a quickly growing secret army that, by year's end, numbered close to 10,000 soldiers in the highlands. By 1964, the CIA was using this massive support network—a system of secret airports, store houses, and training camps—to supply its first bombing missions. Over the next decade, spanning three presidents' administrations, the CIA flew covert missions that dropped more than two million tons of bombs. The Secret War remains the largest covert CIA operation in American history.

Mr. Hart and my father had both been students at the University of California, Berkeley in the 1960s. They never met, but I know that Mr. Hart and Christine marched in the same anti-war protests down Telegraph Avenue and the same rallies at Sproul Plaza on campus. To both, the Vietnam War was a personal specter of the ideological failure of the Left. Along with the rest of the nation, they had listened to Kennedy's speech as a live broadcast. For many Americans, this broadcast would have been the first time they heard of Laos— the first secret about Laos. I was hearing echoes of that secret. Mr. Hart's mispronunciation was a time-marker, like a decomposing isotope, that dated his politics and tied him to this first moment of deception.

In these streets without power lines, the full moon was the brightest lantern. Before the daylight disappeared completely, Chantha and I shepherded the family's water buffalo through the flooded rice fields to the evening pasture. To control grazing, the buffalo was rotated between a morning pasture by the fields and an evening pasture by the house. The low sun smoldered, igniting the tips of the new rice shoots bright yellow. Before us, the road was brilliant as a swath of moonrocks reflecting the last of the sunlight.

"Maa," *come*, Chantha said sweetly, and the buffalo followed us without complaint.

Walking back through the village, Chantha pointed out her neighbors taking evening naps in porch hammocks. She scoffed, "City folks don't nap like that."

All the daylight work was over; it was too dark to weave at the loom, though spider threads caught the angle of the light, each branch a glowing spindle that reminded me of tomorrow's work.

The festival began an hour or two later when the moon was visible above the wat's roof curved like the back of a serpent. The moon rose large and pearled. To light the festival path to the wat, people began to place candles at their gates, and the road started to glow, gate by wooden gate, with rows of tiny flames.

Everyone bought their candles from the same person: the bus driver who came through town each third day on his route from the provincial capital. Chantha and I had taken his bus from the capital to her village. The bus driver's beeswax tapers smelled faintly like honey. It was necessary, Mae told me, that the candles be made of beeswax so that they smelled nice. The candles were quite soft, and Mali easily pressed them into the raised wood grain of the family's fence where they sat upright neatly spaced one for each fence post. Their light was pale saffron, softening, and burned evenly. Mali delighted in lighting them—they were just at her eye-level—but she didn't quite have the coordination to be trusted with a lit candle.

Silavong held the household candle. "Do you want to help, little one?" And, bending down, she wrapped Mali's small child's hands under hers, the two of them together moving the candle from one wick to the next. "Very good."

Out beyond the gate, the crowd moved in moon-bathed blueness, indistinguishable except for the sound, here and there, of raised human voices. That young laugh sounded like Bua, who gathered wild tea in the woods. I also heard two crackling older voices singing. People all along the road took up the song, a bright folk melody with a dance step. Laughing, a group of young women skipped close by and were briefly illuminated in the strips of light, dark, light, dark patterned by our fence posts. I caught a glimpse of heavy woven skirts, long braids decorated with plastic bows, one of them holding unlit sparklers or sticks of incense. There was a procession of people forming in the road, moving toward the village wat—more people than lived in the village, surely, or perhaps the crowd appeared larger at night.

"Go, go, get our fireboats!" Mae waved Chantha and me into the house.

The family formed a line in the front yard, Mae first, then Silavong and Mali, Chantha, and, lastly, the anthropologist. We were each wearing long, traditional skirts, called sihn, sewn by Mae, who purchased manufactured fabric from the bus driver each season in exchange for her hand-loomed silks. The stuff they wove in the village was all sold in the city and was too expensive for them to use for themselves. We had to be careful not to dirty or tear our sihn because Mae intended to sell these upriver after the festival. Mae supplemented her farm income by weaving and sewing clothes but always kept a few high-quality pieces back each season for the family to use on special occasions, like tonight. With Mae's guidance, I chose a sihn that was dark turquoise, the lower half covered by a pattern of stylized water snakes swimming in the shape of the letter Z.

Each of us carried our fireboat, but we didn't light them—not yet. Under Mae's influence, our group moved with significantly more decorum than the crowd. Mae was silent, almost somber. She was already beginning her prayers.

We joined the procession. A few voices rose from the crowd nearby, perhaps recognizing us: "Boun lai hua fai!" *Happy fireboat festival!*

A group of three older women with white dusted faces—party makeup—appeared suddenly near me. They grabbed me by the waist and arms, repeating, "You are beautiful! You are beautiful!" Like ghosts, I wasn't sure if they were trying to frighten me. I didn't fight their grip and only felt a laughing curiosity. Ghosts could be welcome connections to the past in a community where so much was lost to war or leached away to the cities. I looked down to see if the women had feet (some ghosts in Laos don't have feet), but the street was too dark to see their legs. Only their glowing white moon-faces and disembodied, gripping hands. Chantha moved closer to me, shooing away the spectral apparition. "Go bother someone else!"

"But there are no other foreigners in our ban, younger sister!" One of the women pleaded to Chantha without looking at me, still gripping my arm. Foreigners were supposed to bring with them possibilities, connections to overseas wealth. I heard from Silavong that once a group of Japanese development workers stayed in the village, promising new development—and then left without building anything.

Chantha pulled me into the crowd's current, and the moon-faced women disappeared behind us.

A long snake's tongue of white sparks unfurled over the wat wall ahead, followed by more popping and whizzing white firecrackers. Reverse illumination: the wat and the crowd became a single, solid profile as if cut from black paper. In the white flash, the outline of the village roof was briefly visible against the dark sky: two rampant dragons, heads raised, mouths wide baring long teeth. In the day-light, their scales were of small, white river shells pressed into the concrete. Now they seemed made from some brighter stuff, instantaneously gilded by the firecrackers. And their eyes—large, polished red glass marbles—were sparkling with life.

The swollen moon slowly pushed itself higher above the roof.

Past the wat's central building and nearer the river was a flaming boat on a raised bamboo platform. An older monk tended the bonfire—or, rather, stood back and watched it with a satisfied expression which reminded me of Mali lighting the family candles. The fireboat was full-sized and could comfortably have sat a dozen rowers. But it was made from colored tissue paper laid over a spare bamboo frame. The flames tore through it, consuming the colorful paper in sizzling bursts, hungrily. There was hardly any boat left by the time we got there. Visible inside, bamboo troughs of oil were lit at regular intervals along its bottom. It raged, loudly eating the noise of the crowd, and hissed heat. The jagged, white length of the flame was too bright to look at with the naked eye.

Two young novices shepherded a procession of people circling the wat with lit candles. Following Mae, we joined this procession to bless our offerings. I lit my candle on another person's candle, who had lit theirs on their neighbor's candle, and so on. A young girl in a purple sihn came up to light her candle from mine. She paused and stared at me, then began repeating questions in Lao as if she could overcome the language difference with her stubbornness. Her fast, lilting Lao tones were hard to distinguish among the sounds of the festival crowd. I caught some of the young girl's questions: I am Chantha's friend. I have been in Laos for seven months. I am not a farmer. I am from America. Before I could reply with my questions, she disappeared.

Sparklers were distributed throughout the crowd, fizzing from one person to the next. The air was thick with smoke and riven with light like lightening—the paths of fireworks. The world felt eclipsed, smaller, warmer like we had entered a diffusely illuminated white hall. Echoing in that white hall, the laughing clamor of the crowd was punctured by whizzes and pops. People appeared and disappeared into the smoke as if summoned by the proceeding light of their candles. I recognized Old Uncle, gingerly holding two sparklers far in front of him, smiling toothlessly.

One of the monks set off massive corkscrew fireworks, white, that shot up past the moon.

Mali held my hand as the four of us followed Mae out of the circling crowd. Mae steered us past the fireboat, heading for the wat's river gate. The crowd and the smoke thinned beyond the light of the bonfire; there were few people in this part of the village. We passed under the river gate, topped by two entwined dragons, and started down toward the water's edge. Away from the firecrackers and the bonfire, the village became nearly black. We still held our candles, but Mali's and Silavong's had gone out. The moon was hidden but for its pale aureole surrounding a tree. It was difficult to make out our path down the muddy riverbank. My feet felt extremely sensitive, sensing for what I couldn't see. I heard the repetitive slap of our flip-flops sticking and releasing from the mud. Balancing on a log thrown up by the river, my foot slipped, and I began to tip sideways.

Chantha reached out to steady me and then slipped herself, her elaborately woven green sihn now muddied at her knees. Both of our candles went out.

"Oooh, now I will have to wash it!" she exclaimed. Washing meant a bucket in the back field, with the chickens and the buffalo.

"The falang," Silavong used an almost derogatory word for foreigner, "doesn't slip, but the Lao does!" Falang are clueless, totally dependent on their wealth and privilege. Falang don't know how to be poor. "You are spending too much time in the city, Chantha!"

That set Mae and Silavong laughing.

I helped Chantha stand up, saying, "Oh, I am sorry! Thank you for helping me not to fall."

"It's okay," Chantha said to me warmly. "I am glad that only one of us fell."

"I'll help you wash it," I told her.

"Wash mine while you are at it!" Silavong kept up the jokes.

This earned a few appreciative chuckles. All of our candles had gone out.

The river announced itself by its lapping voice, sucking at the bank. I couldn't see its edge until Mae flicked a match and the river reflected the flame in a dozen half-moons. The match kindled Mae's smile, too, in its tiny, pale yellow radius. She quickly lit the candle on her fireboat, then blew the match out before it reached her fingers. Mae relit Mali's candle next, then Silavong's, then Chantha's, and lastly mine.

Mali was already in the river, submerged to her ankles. She leaned down and placed her fireboat in the water, pushing it gently into the current. Her orange sihn was long-since muddy. At first, the little boat came back to her carried by the tongue of the river licking the shore.

Holding my arm, I felt Chantha stiffen. She whispered, too softly for Mali to hear: "It is bad luck if the boat comes back to you—that means none of your bad deeds have been washed away by the river but have been given back to you like a curse." I couldn't see her face clearly in the dark, but her voice showed real concern.

Then the little boat moved in a slow parabola out into the current. Chantha's grip on my arm loosened. The tiny craft elegantly rotated, showing off a crown of white jasmine buds. Its candle illuminated a small surrounding circle of river water. Mali looked at Mae over her shoulder, showed her a grin, and spoke her prayer in a rush: "May everyone come home safely!"

I watched Mali's fireboat move out from the shore and join a procession of other candles floating in the current. The current was swift. Between one person and the next, the first boat was already a small flame far down the river. Dozens were floating past us, including Mae and Silavong's fireboats, all set loose near the village or close by upstream. On the far bank, a large congregation of lights, swarming like fireflies, was moving downstream of the Thai village. The current in the middle of the river was too fast for these small boats to cross, creating an expanse of darkness that separated the two countries. From where we stood on the Lao bank, their lights didn't come to us, but moved past us and far away.

Only Chantha and I still held our fireboats.

She looked at me, somber: "You must pray now. Repeat after me."

She knelt by the water, careful to tuck her skirt into her belt so that it didn't dip in the mud. I knelt beside her. Chantha held her fireboat in front of her with both hands. The small candle flame illuminated her face in the darkness: young and serious, suffused with a healthy light. Two black brows and twin, brown eyes. Narrow nose. Light thinned the new wrinkles around her mouth; wrinkles she fretted over with imported creams. The weave of her black hair caught its flickering shine from the candle. She closed her eyes. I wondered if she was praying to inherit her mother's house in the village or praying for Mali's return from a successful future abroad. The Mekong was part of a water system that spanned the Eurasian continent and the Pacific Ocean, connecting this village to my hometown on the shores of the San Francisco Bay. I knelt next to her and felt suddenly aware of how empty my prayers must be in comparison to hers. I was already blessed with safe returns. I wondered if the dragon would feel the different weights of our fireboats.

Together, we set our boats into the global currents.

"Now, we are modern and take planes to travel. But we still pray to the water dragons for safety. With these boats, we ask that you remove all the suffering from our path—send away sickness, violence, sadness, and poverty. May all who travel be safe. May everyone find their way home."

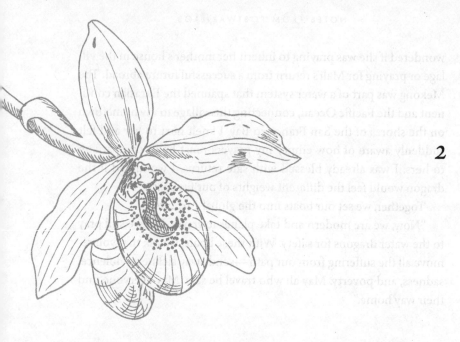

2

"IS IT A CRATER OR A HOLE?"

I pointed at a wide, circular depression in the village's communal rice field, now dry between plantings. The soil along the steep sides was burnt orange but covered at the bottom by flowering yellow brush. Raised earth footpaths between the rice paddies neatly split and circled the hole at a distance of a few feet. The rest of the field was divided into irregular rectangular plots—this was the only circle in the patchwork. During the wet season, the pit was just another irrigation ditch, but when the field was dry its perfect, circular edge appeared cut out from the village, like a scissored hole in a quilt. A stale heat rose from the exposed soil, baked a brittle texture that crumbled into powder, and rustled the bleached weeds at the edges of the field. The network of footpaths extended beyond the rice paddies, flattening and widening into the bald, pounded-open ground between the houses that bordered the field. Interspersed among the houses, fruit trees still green but juiceless, empty of fruit. Nearly identical houses, all thatch-roofed, all single-room and single-story with narrow front porches. None was more significant than any other, or more well-kept. On one of those porches, an older woman watched us with one eye, the other on the red chilies she sorted in a large, flat, woven basket.

"Oh, yes, certainly that's a crater. It's perfectly round. See how there is this little uneven mound all around the edge? That is where the debris landed around the blast." Channarong gestured a circle with his hands, then stretched his arms out broadly, turning to encompass the mud-cracked field and pale, dry stubble of last season's harvest. The field manager for this battlefield survey, he wore a fitted khaki shirt, top three buttons undone, sleeves rolled to the elbows, and army drab cargo pants—dressed very like a soldier. It had been five years since he left the Thai military to become a humanitarian explosives clearance technician. Before Laos, he served on an explosives demolition squad in Afghanistan. We were speaking English, the global language of explosives. He delivered his English with the bottled reserve of an American soldier—sometimes I recognized a West Coast accent, clipped and mixed with military slang. Like many technicians in humanitarian clearance, he was a former soldier who left the military to use his expertise to build peace rather than wage war.

Arms out, his bulky steel-toed shoes stirred up ochre dust as he twirled. He was laughing, looked absurd. Vanida, one of the survey technicians working nearby, turned toward the sound, raising the edge of her wide-brimmed straw hat to watch us. Her hand paused just above her clipboard as if about to record his aberrant behavior on her map.

"It's right in the middle of their field!"

Channarong and I were playing our guessing game: one of us would point to a hole in the ground, and the other would guess if it was a bomb crater or not—and had to back up our guess with evidence. Of course, Channarong was better at it than me. Channarong's ability to identify craters was an essential part of how he surveyed and cleared contaminated villages. During the land survey of this village, he would identify and record the locations of craters as evidence of possible airstrikes. For the last several days, his survey team had been interviewing residents, going over accident and death reports, studying bombing maps from the war, and conducting land surveys of craters, found ordnance, and other military remains. This data would then be used to predict the scope of any future clearance projects in the village. The stakes in this guessing game were high. Channarong the soldier was accustomed to making light of death, which also made him good at his job.

Craters might be filled with debris, or trash, or overgrown with grasses. They might be connected to village irrigation networks and transformed into seasonal fisheries or widened and used as water reservoirs. Filled in with soil, the round stamp of the bomb was often still visible on the flattened earth. He never identified craters in isolation, but always in context with other evidence, such as oral accounts from older villagers who lived through the war. A half-century after a secret war, a lot of this contextual evidence was missing. The military records were classified or inaccurate. The soldiers left or died. No military planes flew overhead. The war was long over, and this one might just be a hole in the middle of their rice field.

We were playing our game in the spare shade of the only tree in the field. A small, scraggly tree with black bark and a thin covering of round, waxy yellow leaves. Its shade was parched, nearly leafless. In the crook of the forked trunk, an orchid bloomed a long spray of tiny white flowers, falling like a pearl necklace. I had positioned myself so that I could see the orchid—I didn't think Channarong had noticed the flower. Life didn't get recorded on these maps; only death, a dot for each explosion that had killed someone in the village. The orchid was absurdly beautiful, pure chance, a little frivolity among the severe work of the survey team. It didn't belong on any of his survey maps.

The survey maps would show that there was a crater in the middle of the rice field.

Channarong was a field manager and also my research liaison: he organized my studies with his teams and was personally responsible for keeping me safe. Wherever I wanted to go, he went first, and I followed. He was an outsized presence in my fieldnotes and a silent observer to many of my research activities. Staying close to each other meant that we had become professional friends— not quite buddies, but good at keeping each other company during long, hot hours in remote villages. Beneath his hardened expertise, I discovered that he had a boyish sense of humor, a little playful and immature. We were good at humor together, but in the way that some comedians are good at humor because they're depressed. Humor was tricky, like a tampered fuse.

Channarong was leaning against the tree trunk, looking at me intently with a trace of something less than jest in his gaze. He took out a blue handkerchief from his front pocket, grimacing in the heat. The handkerchief was already creased with tawny sweat. "Ah, why did your government bomb this? It's just a farming village."

I shook my head at this turn in our game: "That's not fair: I'm an American anthropologist, not an American soldier. You're the soldier!"

Survey technicians in protective vests were visible at regular intervals across the field. I turned away to watch a young man gently swinging his metal detector in front of him; the beeping was softly audible at this distance.

"Okay, but what's your answer—as an American anthropologist?" His grin was baited, friendly, but full of teeth.

I felt our game expanding, the board impossibly vast and suddenly populated with more players. I had heard this question from other bomb techs. My presence and the heat compelled them to ask it, or the long hours bent searching the cracked earth. The foreigner bomb techs asked me *Why did America bomb this?* and *Is this job going to be like it was in Iraq?* and *Is America going to send us more money for clearance this year?* Locals asked of me different sorts of questions, less concerned with explanations and more with the daily necessities of forgiveness. From Vanida, I heard *How can I learn to forgive the Americans who did this?* as if I could tell her how we had learned to forgive ourselves. I had read books of answers to the first questions—history books, political science books, military records, policy reports, and ethnographies of America's wars in Laos and elsewhere—and found far fewer lines written about the second.

"I don't think there was ever anyone who said: bomb this village." I looked at him hesitantly, aware that I was far more comfortable asking questions than answering them. He nodded his head in encouragement. "I've gone through military accounts, and I see a kind of willfully indiscriminate bombing of civilians," and again, I felt myself hesitating. "I don't think they knew what—or who—was actually on the ground beneath their planes. But I also think there's another way in which the war was actually about indiscriminately bombing civilians: the Americans were trying to destroy villages like this so that the Lao state would never flourish if it went communist. Bombing Laos was the beginning of modern counterinsurgency warfare that treats everyday social life as a military target. Villages like this are the battlefield, the places where societies are transformed." The little orchid continued blooming, oblivious.

"You're saying that it doesn't make sense."

I thought about it, trying to see the thing from the point of view of a foot soldier. "Yeah, I guess I am."

His eyes were stern on me, perhaps not satisfied with my answer. Then he nodded his head. "War doesn't have to make sense; it's all violence no matter who is doing the bombing and who is being bombed."

"Yes."

"It's horrid, really, that some people have the power to bomb the shit out of some other people. No one should have that power, but that's the world we live in." His macabre smile returned: "Keeps me employed, eh?"

"It certainly does. With excellent job security."

He neatly folded and tucked away his blue handkerchief. He had completed his move, and the game had returned to its former small proportions: the circumference of the crater before us.

I listened for the soft, regular pings of metal detectors perforating birdsong. I felt my ears tingle. A detector nearby was signaling something underground: its pings sped up, then ceased as the technician set the detector aside to investigate the buried item. If it were a bomb, the technician would call Channarong over to confirm the find. His team used metal detectors to "hear" what was otherwise silent, buried below the surface by time and neglect. Explosions, also, were sounds: when a bomb exploded, it produced a supersonic blast wave that became audible to human ears only at its edges, where the wave had deteriorated into our audible range. At the center of each explosion was a sonic zone of pure destructive silence impenetrable to human senses. A safely audible explosion at four hundred meters was deafening at ten and at one meter, deadly quiet. The soft ping of metal detectors made bombs audible before they exploded. In Channarong's worst-case scenario, the sound of an explosion was the team's first and only clue that a bomb was present.

I could hear other sounds: a repeated machete thud, probably from someone harvesting bamboo nearby; high-pitched laughter, two voices in animated conversation; the wind whisper of the trees leaning into each other. War leaves traces in our lives that are often hard to hear, harder to see. Not explosions, but bursts of life.

"I've worked in theaters of war all over the world: Lebanon, Afghanistan, Mozambique, Sierra Leone, Sri Lanka . . ." He sighed and then pinched his chin with two fingers, a thinking gesture, again serious. His American English was so good it often didn't occur to me that he was translating from one language to another.

"And what do you see?"

"I see that the quality of warfare is changing. It's no longer about big battles, with two clear sides, and armies that meet on an open plain. The battles that I clear are small scale, with many sides and no clear borders. Insurgents in the forest hit with strikes at random. Guerrilla warfare where soldiers change sides many times. There are no more big armies and clearly marked battlefields to be cleared once the war is over."

"So, how do you clear battlefields without borders?" I was thinking about the logistics of clearance and not the deeper meaning of these geopolitical shifts.

He grinned. "Yeah, that's the question. That's what we're trying to figure out."

Channarong was leading an international effort to standardize methods for cluster munition survey and clearance. Laos, the most cluster bombed country in the world, was his laboratory. From roughly 1964 to at least 1973, the United States bombed Laos in secret without the knowledge of Congress or the American public. Before this air war, the United States had managed covert operations on the ground in Laos as early as the 1950s, when a handful of CIA operatives worked in the highlands along Laos' border with Vietnam. The air war was part of a larger Lao civil war between communist and royalist factions, itself part of an even larger regional fight for independence from French and American imperialists. To stop the spread of communism in Southeast Asia, the United States dropped more than two million tons of explosives on Laos—more than the United States dropped on Europe and Japan, combined, during World War II. That's roughly one ton of bombs for every person that lived in Laos. American forces withdrew from Laos when the communist Pathet Lao won control of the state. But the newly independent country was subject to Western trade embargoes and hampered by decades of war, landlocked, and one of the world's poorest and least developed countries. Since the war was a secret, Laos did not receive significant postwar aid, explosives clearance, or refugee assistance. Three decades later, after the fall of the Soviet Union in the 1990s, Laos finally received its first humanitarian clearance teams.

Every clearance box was recorded in one huge, global grid map: count a few thousand boxes over, and Channarong's survey map bumped into a minefield in Myanmar, and from there Bangladesh, then over to Pakistan and Afghanistan; from Iraq and Iran to the airstrikes of Syria, Jordan, Palestine, and Israel; from Syria left to the minefields of Egypt, Sudan and the civil wars of North Africa; and right to the Caucasus and former Yugoslavia, from there up to the remains of the blitz in Europe . . . every battlefield was connected to every other battlefield in Channarong's map. And counting squares in-between, every bit of earth was a future battle waiting to be cleared. This was his soldier's gameboard.

He brought out the master clipboard of grid maps for the village, each grid box hand-colored in red, yellow, green, and blue. When Vanida or another searcher found a live bomb, she marked the corresponding grid box red and then moved on to the next box. If she didn't find any ordnance, she marked that box green. Yellow stood for bomb fragments, blue for ordnance other than cluster munitions. Any found ordnance would be later destroyed in a controlled demolition. The goal wasn't to clear the village but to create a baseline survey of what areas were contaminated with what kinds of ordnance as a way of planning for future clearance. On Channarong's topmost map, about a quarter of the boxes had already been surveyed red or yellow.

"The methods of clearance need to change as the methods of warfare change. Today, there are fewer new minefields and more new cluster strikes," he said.

"What's does that mean for your team?" I asked.

"A minefield has a border: find the first item, and you find the border." He flipped the clipboard to an empty grid map, part of the village the team hadn't yet surveyed. He splayed his hand on the blank map, marking an imaginary minefield. "Then, you can start at the border and clear in, toward the center." He pulled his hand up until his fingers touched in a point, then tapped the center box several times. "It's like filling in a painting: you know how big the canvas is and just paint the inside red, red, red."

"Okay, so how is cluster bomb clearance different?"

He flipped back to the topmost map. A red blob, roughly oval, was emerging from the survey boxes. "Cluster strikes don't work like minefields: there are no clear borders. When you find the first cluster submunition, you treat that like the center and clear out, toward the unknown edge." He tapped one of the boxes at random. "You put a red dot on your map. You spiral out from that first dot until you find the next one, and so on, until you stop finding them—then you have reached the edge of the strike."

He splayed his hand possessively over the half-surveyed strike. "You look for the pattern of red."

I invented this guessing game to encourage Channarong to teach me how to interpret the material remains of war. At first, I hadn't intended to play: I was asking questions to learn to see these old battlefields the way that he saw them. I went out with Channarong and his teams—survey teams, demolition teams, roving teams—and observed how each worked in practice. I soon realized that clearance was already a soldiers' game, and so my questions perhaps inevitably also became a game.

"What about that one: a crater or a hole?"

"Ah, that one's harder. It looks like a dried-up fish pond."

Channarong pointed from one side of the hole to the other, a distance of roughly six meters. The hole was at the very edge of the village's communal rice field. It was dry to its base, revealing a few cans of Beer Lao coated in orange soil. Several of the irrigation channels for the field terminated at the hole, meaning that it would fill with run-off once the rains came. Village residents trapped fish along with the run-off to seed seasonal fisheries. It might be human-made, but for fishing rather than for killing.

"It's certainly big enough! To really know for sure, we'd have to run a metal detector around the edge of the hole to see if the soil contained any bomb fragments from the blast. I'll make sure a searcher does that as part of the village survey."

A man was walking quickly toward us from the village. He was wearing fuchsia plastic flip-flops, an unexpected spot of color flashing, pulsing in the heat shimmering from the exposed ground. When he neared our shaded spot under the tree, he began vigorously pointing to his left. It was several more steps before he was close enough that we could hear what he was saying: "Over there! There is a bomb over there! A bomb!"

Channarong didn't seem particularly worried, so I stayed put. Channarong had surely understood the man's words. He looked vaguely at the man but otherwise hadn't moved: arms folded, leaning against the tree trunk. The man was a little harried, sweating from his walk across the baked field. When he arrived in our shade, he pulled the collar of his faded blue cotton shirt out, fanning himself. The shirt collar was composed of many small worn holes, crenellated like lace. The man's bronze face was bright with exertion. After fanning himself for a few seconds, he began again to wave his arms.

"There is a bomb over there. A bomb." And he pointed a clear injunction. The man looked at Channarong and, not finding what he expected, slowly lowered his pointing finger. His look in my direction was dismissive—one glance from my white face to my wrinkled cotton sihn proved that I was a falang.

Channarong uncrossed his arms and replied in careful Lao: "Yes, thank you for coming to tell us. We already know about that one."

The man drew back his shoulders, standing tall. He continued to explain himself: "I moved it there when I found it in the field six years ago. I didn't sell it or touch it after I moved it."

"Thank you. Don't touch it again."

I was a taken aback by Channarong's dismissal of the man's comments. I saw that this wasn't part of his game—the joviality was gone—because Channarong did not see this man as a legitimate player. In my mind, I thought of myself as a civilian more like the villagers than the clearance staff, but I now understood that Channarong spoke to me as if to a soldier.

"But why haven't you destroyed it . . . ? It is still there." The man's lips tightened, sun-speckled skin wrinkling around his mouth. He leaned back, swaying on the backs of his heels as if Channarong had physically pushed him. "It's your job to destroy bombs."

"We are a survey team, not a clearance team," Channarong kept his pose against the tree, mouthing the Lao phrases without inflection. He was no longer relaxed but stiff as if caught by a live wire. His gaze slipped around as if he couldn't or wouldn't focus his eyes. "A full clearance team will come and clear the whole village later."

A dullness like a shroud came over the man. He shortened, his shoulders slipping down, stooped. He took one step away from us, backward, then another. As he moved out of the shade and into the sun, he thinned at his edges, half-obscured by white sunlight. Now turned completely around, he began his slow walk back toward the houses at the border of the field. Fuchsia flip-flops sparking one, then another, slow step. The color seemed to pale, fast fading as he moved further away. Becoming a mirage, he slipped into the heat and evaporated.

Channarong didn't seem to notice the man's disappearance.

Turning, he pointed back to the village. "Did you see that? This is why this job is so difficult: farmers keep moving the bombs. They're moving the evidence!"

"That one?"

A wide depression, burnt black to the base, and full at the bottom with tarred bottles and plastic bags melted together like pink sugar candy. The smell was lab-produced, cheap toxins smuggled in every plastic bag and every plastic bottle bought at the city market. When lit, the hole sucked oxygen and exhaled acrid blue smoke. A large, black pig was head down in the cold ash, sniffing for her lunch. Her snout stirred the silver dust, sparkling, that then coated her bristled back.

"I assume any big hole around here is a bomb crater," he said.

There was no trash collection, but also little that wasn't repurposed or compostable. Imported foil wrappers; small plastic bottles of sweetened yogurt, empty; the plastic screw mechanism on a stick of deodorant; snapped translucent pull-ties; crescent of a bamboo steamer, bottom burned out; a broken foam flip-flop; cache of blue bottle caps; skewers of bamboo, still oiled with an eaten roast fish; pink plastic bags turned inside out and stuck with grains of sticky rice. The neighborhood collected its trash in this pit and, when it filled, burned it there. The pit was spitting distance from the house Channarong shared with the other senior clearance staff.

The key turned in the latch, and Channarong pulled the door open, bowing forward to invite me inside the house. "You first."

Seated on Channarong's shaded patio, I swirled my limeade with a sliver of bamboo. No ice, but the lime juice was tart and refreshing. Channarong's housekeeper, a woman from the village, had added a little salt with the lime as a tonic for the heat. It was too hot this afternoon to get any clearance work done; the survey team had disbanded at noon.

"How would you compare being in *this* uniform to being in *that* uniform?"

"Oh, they are very different, but the people are often very similar. A lot of deminers are ex-military like me, but we are the people who are trying to get out of the military life. We're the ones trying to get the bombs out of the ground!" He snickered and slouched into his white plastic lounge chair, adjusting his cheap black sunglasses. The back patio was framed on all four sides by a five-foot pink stucco wall. The humming orchestra of cicadas and other insects was constant background noise, thickening the air like fog. Channarong's rental was on the outskirts of town and firmly in the territory of the cicadas, past the range of the street hawkers and peddlers, past the car repair shop, past the police barracks and the town's only checkpoint; here, there were only acres of semi-cleared forest, the road, a communal trash pit, a few stray cows, and a pack of wild dogs.

Passionflowers trailed the top of the pink wall, just opening their blushing buds. The concrete patio was stacked with free weights, organized in little pyramids by weight, and a bench press.

"How did you do that: get out of the military life? You were on a bomb squad in Afghanistan . . ."

"That was five years ago. I saw a lot of action, gunfights, and a few explosions in Afghanistan. I tested myself, and it was good." He said this exactly the way an American would say it.

Then he stopped short, stalled, his mouth open, caught on some unvoiced word. I watched him struggle between languages, his hands fluttering through unfinished sentences hanging in the air and tilting his head this way and that.

"There was a feeling that I didn't like. In the military, you don't have a lot of control, and you don't really know what is going on. It is not a good situation, particularly for feet on the ground. I started to have this feeling: after a few gunfights, I realized that everyone was so close to death all the time. And that it didn't matter; my life didn't matter. The military is a false sacrifice because none of our lives really matter to our higher-ups or the government. The military gave me a balanced perspective on the value of my own life—that I'm in charge of making my life mean something.

"After I left the military, I joined a humanitarian clearance operator working in Laos. I had this training in explosive ordnance disposal, which I learned in the military, and I thought I could do some good by putting it to use to clean up battlefields. I wanted to go home and clean up my father's battles—he had been in the Thai military fighting in Laos."

"The United States and Thailand were allied against communism during the Vietnam-American War," I suggested. "I know that the Thai military sent many tens of thousands of volunteer soldiers to fight alongside American forces in Vietnam."

"Yes, we were allies. Some of these volunteer soldiers worked alongside your secret paramilitary trainers in Laos."

I thought to myself: in the American media, these Thai soldiers were tarred as mercenaries, an insult that still stings for many Thai military and ex-military volunteers. That might have been part of Channarong's upbringing.

He continued. "Now, everyone wants to work in clearance be-cause it's international money—green American money—and there's job security. War ends, and then we come in and clean it up. There's always more war. Everywhere is an old battlefield. But at this particular operator: all the managers were old white men, ex-military from the Gulf War. None of the staff like me were even invited into the meetings!"

"What do you mean: 'like me'?"

"We—the staff—we weren't white, and we weren't ex-military from America or some other global power. The white soldiers never told us about decisions until after they were made. It was a bad situation, just like being in the military! They treated me like nothing, like my expertise didn't matter, like I didn't have choices. So I asked around, found a clearance operator with a better reputation, left that situation, and now here I am!" He raised his glass of limeade. "The field manager for the whole province."

I raised my glass in acknowledgment. The limeade was unfiltered, clotted with lime vesicles like congealed tears. Not sweet, but the unexpected salt cured the bitter.

"That first clearance job: Why do you think they treated you and the other staff like that?"

"It's just plain old racism." There was no irony in his voice, though I remembered how he had dismissed the concerns of the Lao farmer earlier in the day. "That's racism, and that's why I left. I left because if I was going to die as a deminer, I wanted my death to be worth something to my superiors. Now I am proud of being a deminer, and I work for an operator that values me. Because it's a sacrifice."

I heard a gushing from the side yard: the housekeeper had turned the exterior tap, manually filling up the washing machine. My ears were still sensitized. Sounds of Channarong's housemates, other senior clearance staff, could be heard through the open windows above us. Upper window: one-half of a long-distance phone call, muted to round syllables. Lower window: a plastic clatter, like tinker toys, something being taken apart and put back together. There was a giant airdrop bomb displayed by the front door, defused and scrubbed clean to its pocked metal case. Settled into a slight hole, the bomb was upside down with its tapered end pointed to the sky. Its bulging nose was neatly tied with several small braided white *basi* bracelets. Blessing bracelets, given and received at religious ceremonies. A monk or other spiritual leader ritually blesses the white string. The basi strings tied around one's wrist cannot be easily discarded and are often carefully retied to a tree as a supplication to the tree spirit to pass the blessing on to heaven. I wondered: Who in heaven will receive the blessings tied around a bomb?

"What are you sacrificing?"

One hand gestured a circular motion that encompassed himself, the patio, the defused bomb, the free weights, the pink house. "My life, I am sacrificing my life. My wife doesn't like that—she wants me to quit."

A loud, round sound burst over the patio wall. A popping sound, like a massive blown-up balloon ripped to squeaky rubber shreds.

Channarong came half out of his chair.

"Was that an—?"

Crater or a hole?

He looked at me, mouth slightly open in a small, vulnerable oval. A vibrant color crept up his cheeks, the rising pink of panic.

I watched him with a craving like hunger—hungry for his sensitivity. I wanted to hear the way that he heard, and I wanted to feel his fear. I wanted to see the outline of craters, each circle crisp and shining darkly as a solar eclipse, the way that Channarong saw them. I thought of Christine, who had marched against this war and whose anger had always seemed so much sharper than mine, more focused and somehow also more justifiable. She was angry about the war; I was merely researching it with a scholar's detached objectivity. When I shared my research articles with my dad for feedback, she would cross out the word *experience* and replace it with *suffering*; she would cross out *bombing* and write *slaughter*. Anger about war is a specific type of anger that points out the excess, the unreckoned violence we inflict on each other. In the vending machine of global mass media, it is a privilege to express real anger about the war, any war. Calm and detached books, news reports, and radio programs about war shook her, rattled my dad's anger out of her like an upside-down saltshaker. But I didn't have those reflexes—I was still firmly in my seat, my glass of limeade in my hand. I tongued the salty-sour juice, tasting it like sweat.

What was I afraid of?

A break in. My research materials being stolen.

The soldiers at checkpoints. The tiny surveillance holes in the ceiling of my Vientiane apartment, and what that meant.

Men. Being harassed and assaulted.

My mother. The familiar anger of my mother.

Slowly, Channarong leaned back into his chair and crossed his ankles in pantomimed relaxation. A controlled breath. Then he laughed, once, mocking himself: "Ah, no, that came from the road. A motorbike crash; it sounds nothing like a bomb. It's too hot, no teams are working this afternoon."

We sat a few breaths in silence. He pulled out his blue handkerchief and swabbed his forehead and neck with slow, circular strokes.

There were other players in our game: Channarong's family in Vientiane, including his wife, Lani, and their newborn daughter, Noi. He lived in Vientiane one week out of every four. The family house was in a new, as yet unpaved, urban development in a zone often left off of maps of the city. The district was mostly half-roofed houses and neat stacks of red bricks. Chickens picked through the open sewage ditch that was the main link between the sprawl and the city center. Ringed by fields on all sides, their neighbors tended small plots to supplement city salaries. The family house was in progress: the first floor mostly finished, with an unbuilt back room planned for guests. The back door opened onto nothing: a concrete square the shape of their future. An avocado tree grew in the rear yard, foreign; Lani had shown it to me like it was my relative. In Vientiane, Noi was eating her first real foods, mashed roasted eggplant, sticky rice, ginger broth. Her first words were "khao" and "mae," the Lao words for *rice* and *mother*. She didn't yet know the word for father.

The sound of the crash shifted the gameboard between us. I wasn't afraid of explosions, and that meant that in this moment I was the one with the power. I said, "You are sacrificing more than just your own life."

"Yes, I know that." He removed his black-rimmed sunglasses and closed his eyes, face up to the blue sky. Breathed out a long, hissing breath. Then opened his eyes, looking up. Blue: the color of a clearance box with a mortar shell: a clean, cloudless blue. "My life means so much more now. It was so easy to sacrifice myself when I was a simple soldier."

That phrase, "simple soldier," came with a self-deprecating snicker. He put his sunglasses back on.

"But now, I don't want my wife to be by herself, and I don't want my daughter to grow up without a father. I am so proud of that—of being a father! But I don't know how to be a father and also be here doing this job. I am thinking of changing to an office job, something in the city."

"Then you'll finally be out of uniform."

"Yes, no more bombs. People's lives are at stake, you know?"

Over the wall came the demanding honks of a truck—the crash was blocking traffic. This was the only paved road in the region, a straight black tar line across Laos from Vietnam to Thailand. The rumble of large, idling engines could be heard beneath human voices, talking rapidly. The sounds resolved into coordinated cries of "push!" and a metal screech as something substantial was moved out of the traffic lane. A low thud. I could nearly hear the rising gray road dust, thickening in the heat that slicked the asphalt, now settling over the abandoned motorbike.

I walked the same road in the evening and found irregular pieces of blue plastic and translucent red and white lenses scattered over the road like large confetti. The lanes were stripes of gray and tawny dust, painted by the wheels of the cars, now marred by a diagonal curve of black skid. The motorbike was pushed into the drainage culvert, bending the long arms of lotus growing even in the dry season, broad-leafed and luminous green above the slip of condensed yellow slime and offal. A pack of wild dogs investigated the wreck, barking as high and thin as their bellies, sniffing the still hot tires. Trucks drove by without stopping; they transported primeval timber furred like the preserved remains of mammoths. Much later, in the cool of the early evening, the town's only police officer came and laid his measuring tape upon the road. He noted the length of the skid in his report.

3

FOR MY EIGHTEENTH BIRTHDAY, my dad's partner Cybele gave me the power to kill. She handed me a nondescript card, held out with both hands at waist height, gripping the upper corners between her thumbs and forefingers, the way soldiers hold folded flags at funerals, and said, "If you ever need someone dead, you call this number, okay?"

I took the card and opened it, no envelope. The cover was of a bird on the rung of a cute birdhouse. Inside, I read an unfamiliar phone number neatly written in Cybele's last-century cursive. No other descriptions or instructions. No "Happy birthday! Love, Cybele."

"You ever in danger, you call," she said and pointed her finger at me as if to pin the instructions to my body. "Don't lose that card."

Standing just behind Cybele, my dad, Christine, mouthed, *It's an honor.*

I believed her: it was an honor to be given this power, the honor of a soldier trusted with a weapon. I knew it was a power that I would never use. When I was growing up, Cybele was the only living member of my immediate family who was a veteran, but by the time I was born, war had settled into the everyday contours of life in America: plastic toy guns on the playground; army advertisements in movie theaters; war reportage in the daily news; a friend's father in a wheelchair; and later, when I went to university, military funding for research programs. I grew up in the shadow of America's global war on terror, our forever wars in the Middle East and elsewhere. I possess no memories of living in an America at peace. I held the Hallmark card to my chest with both hands and said, "I'll keep this safe."

I never saw Cybele's gun, but at that moment, I imagined it: oiled black, polished, and shining. I imagined her taking it apart laid neatly on a white towel, the pieces unfamiliar to me; then, before I could touch its insides, she'd clean them and deftly put the gun back together. Click, click, click. It was issued during her service in Vietnam.

I never met Cybele when she was a man, but I had seen her army photos. "I was a handsome soldier," she said when she showed me the black-and-white headshots, the photographs edged in a faded border the color of tobacco stains. Her hair in the photo was a luxurious, enviable black, held with pomade, parted on the side like Cary Grant. She looked a bit like him, too, but with burnished bronze skin, black hair, and a more regal nose. Hers was struck off a Roman coin: aquiline. After her gender transition, she had gotten cosmetic surgery to make her nose more feminine. The soldier in the photo no longer looked like her—I had never met that man and never seen that soldier's gun. Cybele had sighed nostalgically as if looking at photos of an old family home.

My memories of Christine as a man were easy for me to revisit: these memories felt well-loved and clear. Dad's life was less touched by violence, and I had no sense of discontinuity or rupture between versions of herself. I still recognized my dad in my family photographs, or rather I recognized a woman that was always there in those photographs, hidden inside of her. I knew little about how

Christine met Cybele, but I sensed that there was a healing core to their relationship: an effort to make themselves whole for each other. When Christine had transitioned, she had told me, "No matter how I change, I'll always be your dad," and that felt true.

Cybele was the last surviving member of her military unit. Everyone else died in Vietnam or committed suicide after the war, back in the States. In a way, the male version of herself had died there, too. There was no one left who had known her as a soldier.

Who would pick up if I called the birthday card number? Who stood by that phone, waiting for the sign of death? Was it that soldier in the photograph—the version of Cybele that I never met? It was hard for me to imagine who might be on the other end—of the phone line, of the gun. Past the muzzle, the image blurred. In the aftermath of violence, memories and imagined things settle into the uncomfortable spaces between one person and the next. I didn't know how to make a connection to that other, more brutal world, but I kept listening for its call.

Crumpled boats from the Fireboat Festival still littered the riverbank when Chantha suggested that the family take a trip across the Mekong to Thailand.

"Everything is for sale in Thailand," she said, trying to entice me. "And nothing for sale here."

In my field notebook, I had made a complete list of what Bua, the tea forager, sold in her front-porch shop: wild tea by the scoop, buckets of small black snails, bunches of bitter herbs tied with strips of reed, quivering cages of crickets. She sold single-use packets of soap, shampoo, and conditioner in pearlized plastic beads hung in necklaces from the eaves of her house. Unregulated medicines of dubious provenance whose packages read like Rosetta stones of English, French, Chinese, Russian, and Thai. Disposable, cheap, small things that could be easily transported by motorbike from the city or the forest. Under the communist state, there was little financial policy or infrastructure to support trade in these villages. Bua sold unbranded cigarettes and, during the Festival, homemade clay fireworks. The fireworks preserved the fingerprints of their makers in their hardened but unfired clay casks, a memory of human touch, fragile identities ready to explode. I held a firework in my hand, turning it just so, until my fingers pressed into the trace of another person's prints.

For Chantha's family, the border between Thailand and Laos was a figment of the government, illusory and invisible on the ground. There was a sense that the border was as liquid and changing as the river itself. And the suggestion that a government official could manage that liquid border—you might as well control the river— sounded foreign and unfamiliar. Before the French, the kingdoms of mainland Southeast Asia had no borders and instead radiated out from capital cities, like lamps, whose influence shaded out the further one walked from the city's center. At the edges, the power of one king might blend with the power of another: some people held citizenship in multiple kingdoms, and people might move between kingdoms to take advantage of lower taxes or other privileges. Today in Laos, people owned houses but not necessarily the land beneath. It was possible to walk across Chantha's village in any direction without being bothered by a fence, only a few of which sliced through fields and homesteads. People were expected to roam where they pleased. The family's chickens had no coop; they flocked to the pond during the day and roosted under the houses in the evening.

And through the village ran the road: it began across the far border in Vietnam, cut through the mountains, fell downslope to the village where Channarong's survey team worked, then to the provincial airport where it was briefly paved, and crossed the valley to the village, sweeping past Chantha's house until it met the river and turned north to the capital city and from there finally crossed the Friendship Bridge (and passport control) to Thailand. That was the long way around, Chantha explained, or we could ferry a boat a half-hour across the river.

The sense I got from Chantha was that river crossing was like a trip into a parallel world, a more prosperous life waiting on the other side. The feeling was like visiting an older sibling with vastly better personal fortunes. On the other side of the river, Chantha and her family might have lived out a different history: significantly more developed and wealthier than its neighbors, Thailand held the distinction of being the only state in the region that was never colonized by a Western power. Thailand still had its king.

Chantha's plan was a problem for me because I wasn't an easy border-crosser. In California, I grew up with border walls and militia and night crossings, the dead abandoned in southern deserts. I wasn't keen on illegally crossing borders and didn't particularly want to go to Thailand. For me, Thailand lacked the allure of alternative fortune. But I didn't know how to say no in Lao. I knew a good many ways to say yes: jao (*okay*); eu (*yup*); doi kanoi (*respectful yes*); dee lai (*very good*); maen (*correct*); dai leow (*of course*), etc., but not a single way to say no. I had looked in my dictionaries—one dictionary had no entry at all, and the second had an entry for baw, a word I had heard used as a negation (baw sep, *not delicious*) but never as a conversational no. This linguistic handicap earned me hours of harmless small talk, acres of unwanted vegetables at the market, and a calendar of accepted social invitations to strangers' parties. The endless yeses were a burden. I do not know why I chose this moment to say no; perhaps my resistance was a deep-seated result of being born with borders?

When Chantha and I were alone, cleaning dishes by the spigot in the back yard, I confessed: "Okay, Chantha, I don't really want to go to Thailand, but I don't know how to say no in Lao."

"Oh!" Her face softened, and she reached out to put a soapy hand on my arm. We were up to our knees in joyful weeds fed by the water from the spigot, which leaked.

"That's because people don't say no in Lao," she explained to me. "It's considered rude. You must be careful not to put the other person in the role of offering something unwanted because it makes them look bad. You can say no if you make sure that the other person doesn't feel embarrassed."

"So I could say: I don't feel comfortable crossing the border to Thailand, but I encourage you to go without me?"

She patted more soap on my arm, "Yes, very well done."

The next evening at dinner, after the family returned from their river trip, we gathered on cushions at a round, woven table-tray packed with leftovers saved from the day before: plates of sautéed greens, spicy relishes, fried snails, scrambled eggs, and pickled onions. The rice was steaming in a separate bamboo container on the floor.

Handing me a bowl of garlic relish, Silavong asked: "Chantha told me that you are training to be a doctor?"

"Yes, but not a medical doctor. I am training to be an anthropologist."

She bowed from one side to another, saying with her ample body that both were good. Silavong was at least double the weight of Chantha—I had the suspicion that Chantha's frame would fill out as she aged. "If you want, I will teach you how to blow blood."

I thought I had misheard and looked with confusion from her to Chantha. Chantha nodded, yes, I had heard right. She leaned in and whispered to me: "She means local medicine. Silavong is a maw-phi, a *spirit doctor*. She knows blood blowing, a kind of medicine of breathing. She is asking if you want to learn—this is an honor."

Silavong was steadily looking at me. She spoke again in a low voice, nearly threatening. "I must warn you: blood blowing only works if everyone is a good Buddhist and believes in the method. The heart of blood blowing is prayer and belief. The patient must believe in it. The practitioner must believe in it, or it is worse than dangerous. So I will only teach you if you believe in it and don't just want to know for your cultural study."

I let her invitation rest for a breath, considering. Oh, I felt such yearning! What a research opportunity: to apprentice to a shaman!

But, mindful of Silavong's warning, could I sincerely believe in her methods without sharing her beliefs?

The subject of my being a good Buddhist was an ongoing debate within Chantha's family. Their general assumption was that I must, in my heart, be a good Buddhist because I tried to live my life according to principles that the family practiced: nonviolence, compassion, and mindfulness. I had a degree in Buddhist studies and had read religious texts in English translation. My father had taken orders at a Buddhist monastery in the American Midwest, where she had served for many years. I was also, and Chantha felt that this was very important, a pacifist studying postwar reconstruction. "You are trying to reduce suffering in the world, which is the central goal of Buddhism," she had told me with her palms together in prayer over her heart. Chantha maintained that I could be a Buddhist without practicing the prayers or believing in the tenets of the faith, such as reincarnation and karma, because "Buddhism is like a science for living well. It isn't a religion that one has to necessarily believe." Apparently, Chantha and Silavong had discussed their assessment of my Buddhism while they had been out shopping. But I could not, in my heart, call myself a good Buddhist.

This was not the first time I had been asked to be a healer. I recalled a conversation with a Lao medical doctor back in California, before I left for my last year of fieldwork.

Gray-haired Doctor Sawm and I greeted each other with bows at the door of his medical practice, and then he invited me into his private office. Gold-framed photos of smiling girls in brocade sihn— his grandkids, I assumed—flanked his leather office chair. He told me that he had had a dream the night before: about a doctor who would visit him and ask for his blessing to go to Laos and heal the wounds of his ancestors, many of whom had died in the war. He felt that I must be that doctor.

"We are all moving through this life, and the Buddha has brought you to me for a purpose; perhaps we have lived many lives together before," he began in a warm tone, as if we had known each other for many years. "You have been foretold to me. It is my experience as a medical doctor that some wounds cannot be healed with medicine. As I am sure you know in your profession, some social ills cannot be fixed in one life, or by one person. Tell me, do you think an anthropologist is also a kind of healer?"

I demurred, unwilling to accept his family's burdens. But feeling my own youth and inexperience, I was also afraid that he might be right. His last words—the question—almost struck me like an accusation, though I could tell he meant his words with kindness. I left without asking for his blessing and never again spoke to Doctor Sawm. I did not know how to hear his words rightly, I think.

Could I hear Silavong's words rightly, these many months later? Would I again turn down the offer to be a healer? Considering her invitation, I went over what I knew about her shamanic practice: Silavong was a border-crosser, crossing geopolitical borders between nations, and crossing spiritual borders between the realms of the living and the dead and the spirits that were neither. Her practice was split by the Mekong River, with clients in the villages on both banks. The nearest clinic or pharmacy was in the provincial capital, several hours driving inland, and no one in the village owned a car. Everyone else had to go the long way around, but Silavong knew the quickest path to the spirit world.

Once, Cybele offered to teach me how to shoot a gun. I turned her down. I knew I couldn't shoot a gun, even in pretend.

"Aunt," I said with a small, formal bow, "I am honored by your offer. I am interested in studying blood blowing—but am not a Buddhist, and I do not believe in your method. I thank you for your warning."

She nodded, clearly disappointed, and quickly moved the dinner conversation on to other things. I felt uncertain and hoped that I had said no without embarrassing her.

Thinking about it that evening while writing up my fieldnotes, I sadly reflected that I had done the right thing by turning down

Silavong's offer. I had twice turned down the offer to be a healer. And, as I felt earlier with Doctor Sawm, Silavong's question had stirred up feelings of uncertainty about my role in the community and the value of anthropology as a reparative practice. I was a border-crosser of a different type. What if I had turned the question back onto the shaman: I'll teach you anthropology, but only if you believe in my methods? Reflecting on this, I knew that I wouldn't have given her the choice to say no.

The morning almsgiving was held in the open grounds surrounding the gilded river wat. The village women took turns providing food for the lone monk who now lived there, plus his small rotating coterie of young novices sent by their mothers to learn about the Buddha. Mae owned a set of stacking metal food canisters specifically for this purpose. But this week, in celebration of the Fireboat Festival, the morning almsgiving was much larger: more like a holiday donation drive. The village women had been collecting packaged food and other goods for weeks and were dropping them off in the morning along with their prepared, hot meals.

We were at one of these donation drives at the wat, sitting on our heels on a woven mat waiting to receive blessings from the monk. On some point of pride, Mae had made sure we were among the first people to arrive. She and Chantha had prepared a basket of toothpaste, toothbrushes, soap, and face towels, topped with a container of fresh sticky rice and a pack of incense. This was why the family had gone shopping in Thailand—you couldn't buy good toothpaste in the village.

Out the window of the wat, I could see a cobalt sky dulled to an ashen blue-gray where it veiled the spires of the cemetery shrines, clustered together, some leaning crooked or crumbling. These shrines were cone-shaped structures with a cavity at their middles, sometimes protected by a small door, for storing urns of cremated remains or other relics, and a small altar for offerings. Much of the day's donations were marked for funeral offerings to the deceased of this cemetery. A laundry line of monks' robes was strung, bright orange, between two funeral spires.

Silavong patted me on my leg and pointed to a man who was just passing through the dragon gate from the village: "Look, look, he is blind!"

I glanced briefly over, feeling that to look would be rude, but as soon as I turned away, Silavong patted my leg again, "Look, I want you to see him!"

The older man was wearing cheap plastic sunglasses and clutching the arm of a relative. His head was slightly bent to the side as if he heard better in his left ear.

How long was I supposed to look?

I watched the older man being guided over to another mat, not far off from ours.

Nearly as soon as I glanced away, Silavong tapped my leg again. "Look, look at her leg!"

A woman was coming through the dragon gate, shambling on a hugely swollen, purple leg. The skin at her ankle was scaled with dried excretions. A very young woman, wearing an attractive sihn and a bejeweled sandal on her well leg.

"Look, that one, she gets epilepsy."

There was also a woman missing an ear. And a child who had lost their voice after a high fever. A couple that could not conceive ever since they had snubbed the funeral rites of a wealthy aunt. A father and his son, both with a rash on their left arms. A young man who wore makeup, when he could afford it. An older woman whose three sons had all died and left no one to pray for her.

Silavong knew these private truths, this pageant of misfortunes, because she was the village shaman.

"Look, look at them," she said to me and pointed, again and again, at the people coming through the dragon gate. And though it made me uncomfortable, I looked.

I remember finding a tiny rocket on the windowsill of dad's latest studio apartment. The little thing was only two inches high sitting on its base of four fins. Its nose was smooth but tarnished with fingerprints as if it had been kept in some small boy's pocket. I could already see it among my dinosaurs and giraffes—it was the same scale, the size of things that fit easiest into my child's hands. The fins were sharpened as if sliced from razors.

"I found a rocket!"

Dad reached out to take the thing from me as if I might hurt myself. "Oh baby . . . !" But then she tempered and didn't know what to say.

Cybele put a hand on dad's arm and pulled her back, whispered, "If she doesn't know what it is, don't tell her."

There was a hard look between them that I pretended not to see. I saw Cybele's gaze harden and then soften. I understood she was protecting me from something.

"Let her have it," she pleaded to my dad, "Let her think it is a toy."

I kept it among my dinosaurs, and later, my jewelry. I was a teenager when I realized what it really was—a bullet.

This gentle ignorance was one way that Cybele protected me. Her worldly knowledge was a kind of violence, something that she didn't want to know, and that she tried to keep from others. The knowledge often came out of her of its own accord as if she was possessed by the soldier she had once been. There were things that she couldn't see straight on because she had seen them with a soldier's eyes. Cybele said that ghosts were shadows, black shapes that moved at the corners of her vision, barely visible but there. They wanted to be seen, but only at the edges.

I walked back to Chantha's house from the wat by myself, taking a longer route through the fields. On my return, I found on the windowsill a thick braid of beeswax candles, partially melted. The wax was a dusty, dun-colored yellow still sticky with traces of honey. The wax stems had been plaited together and then lit and burned as if a single candle. There were five strands in the plait—one for each family member. I touched marigold petals preserved beneath the half-congealed wax drippings, still perfect orange and tear-shaped petals, hard and visible under thin wax like a layer of skin. I knew that the braided candle was a protective object meant to materialize the interconnections and mutual support of the five family members. I imagined the people I had seen at the wat as if each were trailing a line that connected them to every other member of their family and the village.

Inside the house, there was a smell of flowers and of incense. But the house seemed empty. Since the windows had no screens or glass, the flies flew in and out of the parlor like uncertain guests. Next to Mae's sewing machine, her tailoring orders littered the floor, scraps of people-shaped fabric that were empty and waiting to be put on.

"Aunt Silavong?"

"Over here," she said and invited me to sit next to her on cushions in the rectangle of light from the open window. Her mouth was relaxed, and her brow smooth, and I knew she'd been meditating. By her side, she was burning incense in a tiny porcelain bowl.

Nearly as soon as I sat down, there was a rustle at the front door.

A gray figure appeared against the light; I saw that a man had stopped with one foot on the threshold. His presence was like smoke blown indoors, a smear in the air, a large shadow cast by a smaller shape. I had heard that Silavong's newest patient was a man from a nearby village suffering from possession by a ghost-relative killed in the war.

Silavong saw the man hesitate and, smiling, waved him inside. "Sabaidee, Bounmi! Come in and let me talk to you."

Then she gestured to me, sitting next to her. "This is my guest. She's an anthropologist studying the war. She would be interested in your story."

He bowed to me respectfully. His voice, when he spoke, was higher and lighter than I expected. I realized that he was young, perhaps Chantha's age, but that his sadness made him seem older.

"Do you prefer English? I am very good."

"I do, if that is comfortable for you?"

"Yes, yes. I enjoy the practice," he said in his young man's voice. "Sometimes, I work with the American clearance teams."

I nodded my thanks.

I was learning that there was an invisible border between Silavong's shamanic therapy and my anthropological research. The border wasn't steady, or easy to find, and was more like the lighted territory between two lamps. I wasn't familiar with this territory. I felt like I was trespassing—but I sensed that Silavong still wanted me to be her apprentice. We were negotiating something that I only partly understood.

"Bounmi is a war scrap trader. He sells bombs," Silavong said by way of introduction.

"Is that how you came to work for the clearance teams?" I asked in English, sensing that this was expected of me.

"Yes," he bowed forward politely acknowledging my question. "I am known in this area as an expert. I know where the bombs are and the fallen aircraft. There are many ruins in these forests."

"Would you tell me about how you came to that profession?"

The man closed his eyes, perhaps collecting his memories.

"I learned from my father, who learned from his father during the war. My grandfather was a soldier for the Pathet Lao in these mountains." The Pathet Lao were the communist revolutionaries backed by their neighbors in China, Vietnam, and the USSR and fighting against the American-backed monarchy. "The Soviets taught the Pathet Lao soldiers how to dismantle and demolish bombs. When my grandfather returned to our ban, he saw that the war was not yet over and the land was full of bombs. So he taught his son, my father, how to make the land safe. And my father taught me."

"Will you teach your son, then?"

"Yes. The knowledge to dismantle bombs is in the blood of my family for generations. This metal is inside us: it is like the iron in our blood. I received it from my father and I will pass it on to my son." He pounded his fist over his heart several times for emphasis. Again, I had the impression of a youth hidden inside the mantle of a much older man.

"Kow jai, kow jai," I confirmed in Lao, meaning *I understand*, a phrase that literally translates as *it is in my heart*.

I was performing some role in Silavong's ritual, but I didn't understand what role.

Bombs leaving a metal trace in the blood of generations: What kind of medicine heals these wounds? Could I possibly help to heal this?

Silavong took the young man's hands in hers and began to breathe deeply, then exhaled her breath over his palms in a hiss through tight lips.

Then she stopped, seeming to remember that I was there, and asked me in Lao, "Would you make us some tea? Just two cups."

Confused but recognizing my exit, I went into the backyard kitchen and set a pot over the smoking mouth of the coal stove that I kindled from below with a match. I leaned against the kitchen counter, looking through the back door to the pair in the sunlight of the parlor window. Silavong was gently hovering her hands, palms down, over Bounmi's body. I turned away from the scene, feeling it was rude to look.

I was still and silent as if any movement might disturb Bounmi's exorcism. The bodies of ghosts could be easily moved in the air, like particles of dust. They wanted to be seen, but at the edges of things. Silavong might invite the ghost-relative to possess her: I imagined that older man's voice coming out of Silavong's mouth, her comfortable limbs tightening into the body of an anguished soldier.

Distracted, but trying not to show it, I sorted the tea leaves from the stems and selected long, intact leaves that would bloom beautifully in their cups. The babbling boil gave off a wordless plume of steam.

I brought out a tray with two cups, laid it by their cushions, and then quietly left.

✿

I went over this scene with Chantha while the two of us walked the family's buffalo to the evening pasture, as was our chore each night. The exchange with Bounmi had felt staged: it was too much of a coincidence that he spoke English well, and that Silavong had invited me to sit with them only to quickly ask me to leave. I was sure that I was missing the context to understand what was going on and why Silavong had wanted me to hear only that first part of Bounmi's story.

Chantha thought for a moment and then said: "Do you know how the story of the three brothers ends?"

This surprised me: I hadn't realized that there was more to their tale, and I wondered why Chantha had waited to tell me the rest of it. What did the three brothers' story have to do with Bounmi's story?

"I only know the part that you told me before—about the airplane."

The brothers began to occupy the air as if Chantha had invoked them with her words. I had assumed they were fictions, made-up men, but now I realized my error. I wondered why I had not thought before to ask her how their story ended. It upset me more than I could understand.

After the brothers' success with melting and selling the downed airplane, Chantha continued, they became more ambitious in their war scrap trading. They searched ever more dangerous parts of the jungle and took jobs with larger bombs that other traders refused to handle. "They were like three fighting cocks, looking for danger." A friend in the village tipped them off that a bomb, at least a few hundred pounds of explosive, was lodged in a creek a half-day's walk into the jungle. The three brothers set off with their machetes, their metal detector, their shovels, and supplies for a three-day trip. They found the bomb: as long as each of them was tall and fatter than the three of them put together. They had defused bombs of this size before and had perhaps gotten overly confident in their skills: the bomb exploded. Back in the village, Silavong and the other villagers heard the blast reverberate through the river valley.

"The sound was a crack in the air," she said, "like the start of a landslide in the mountains, or like closing your eyes and seeing only bright whiteness."

Mae, in her role as the village chief, organized a rescue team composed of Silavong and two young women known for their physical strength. The rescue team sighted the plume of smoke as a guide and followed it into the jungle. They found at its base a bald bowl of earth and a creek in shambles, the watercourse pushed several meters to the southeast. There were no bodies—they had been vaporized by the blast—but the would-be rescuers did find a few traces of the three brothers: a machete blade shorn in silvery pieces, a shoe with its sole blown off, and an arm. Not knowing what belonged to which brother, the three women carefully wrapped the blade, the shoe, and the arm in homespun cloth and carried them to the wat.

"We were afraid that if we did not properly memorialize the brothers, they would return as angry ghosts to set off more bombs," Chantha explained. Under pressure from the villagers to prevent the dangerous ghosts from wandering, Silavong decided to treat the blade, the shoe, and the arm as the physical remains of the brothers. A respectful conceit to soothe the dead. Knowing that the ghosts of the brothers would be wandering the jungle, angry and afraid, she performed a ceremony to call back their spirits, asking them to be at peace at the wat, where she promised that the monk would pray over them.

"There have been no explosions since then."

"And when was that?"

"About five years ago."

When we returned from the buffalo pasture, Silavong was waiting: "Would you like to interview me tomorrow? I could tell you what I remember about the war."

For this invitation from her, I only knew how to say yes.

I imagined the fire, the house burning, as Silavong told it to me. The house was burning because she was telling me about her childhood during the war.

"I remember seeing the house on fire, the roof burning," she said. "The roof was made of grass, and the walls were woven bamboo around a wooden frame. The flame peeled the walls away so that I could see the room where my mother, Mae, and I slept, I could see it as if through a large window. This was before Chantha was born; she was born after the war."

Chantha nodded. She touched her fingers to my leg and then removed them, like the brush of a leaf.

"The house was flaming brightly colored red and gold. And the garden was burning: our mother's garden of vegetables for us to eat, so I knew that we would have no food. The tomato vines on their trellis turned into pillars of flame. Our mother had dug a hole near the house, almost as deep as we were tall, just big enough so that the three of us could crouch inside it. With a round roof woven of grass that we could just pull on and off. That was where we hid from the bombs."

Silavong lifted her hand up to the height of her ears—how deep her mother dug. Her eyes drifted away from me to look at Chantha, inviting her niece into the memory. "They were falling from the sky. I remember they were yellow and round, and they fell without exploding. They were about this big."

Still looking to Chantha, she cupped her hands into the shape of a cluster submunition. About the size of an orange.

It occurred to me that Silavong had never told this story to Chantha before—and that was why Chantha had not told me about the craters or known that her village had been bombed. I realized that Silavong was asking me to facilitate sharing this story with her niece: asking me for the interview and asking her niece to help translate. I understood that it was a story that Silavong needed to tell indirectly. I wasn't a shaman, but in that moment, I felt that I was holding open a space for them. Chantha's translations and Silavong's memories mixed in my mind; they were both speaking at the same time, telling the same story but in different voices, the second voice younger and more frail.

"One of them fell right next to our hole. I could see it through the grass roof." I imagined that slice of air, Silavong's childhood compressed to a thin view of fire. The roof was fragile as cardboard, combustible, between them and the burning sky. The acrid, roasting smell of a life lit by violence. In my mind, the garden was silent; all sound pulled from the scene as fire pulls oxygen. I had asked Silavong: What do you remember about the war?

"I did not know that they were supposed to explode—I didn't understand that they were what had lit the house on fire. There were so many of them that didn't explode. Our grass house burned down, but afterward, we moved into the dirt house."

"You lived in the hole?"

"Yes, there was nowhere else to live. Our mother gathered the bombs from the garden, where her eggplants used to grow, and carried them to the woods. I don't know what happened to them after that." Her charred garden, cinder and ash that fed the yellow bombs, round and fertile, the fruit of war. Chantha was watching her aunt with a look of sympathetic alarm.

"They never exploded?"

"No, they never exploded."

I could not bring myself to ask anything more. I let my handwriting catch up with the silence. My private shorthand was a looping alphabet of mostly consonants that I adapted from my public school cursive, my training in calligraphy, and symbols borrowed from legal and medical notation. I learned the medical notation from my mother, who had worked in a clinic and needed to translate nearly indecipherable doctors' notes. All of these personal and family practices were distilled in my fieldworkers' shorthand. Every letter flowed into the next, and my sentences were long, sinuous lines interrupted by twists and slashes, and bent at the margins. I scribbled a few quick descriptions of the scenery, the sounds of the house: the splash and laughter of two kids at the laundry, the shuttle of a neighbor's loom, the crackle of a garbage fire. Clink of our three teacups on the tiled porch.

After some time, Silavong said: "That is all that I remember of the war." And then, in a formal voice that seemed to ritually end the interview, she spoke a familiar Lao adage: "Food that is not eaten will rot. Memories that are not told are forgotten."

Most of the people that I met in Laos where like Chantha and did not know much about the war. If they did know about the nine years of bombing, they did not know why. I saw in my mind a map of postwar Laos: on the back of a paper napkin, an aid worker drew the shoehorn shape of Laos and then added a thick line down the middle of the country, from tip to tip, dividing the lowlands from the mountains. Two sides. She put her finger on the lowlands, the side of the capital city and the ethnic Lao ruling elite: "On this side, ignorance." And then put her finger on the mountains, the side of the more ethnically diverse highland communities, usually poor and underresourced. The Ho Chi Minh Trail, the military supply route to North Vietnam, ran through these mountains and was a heavy bombing target during the war. "On this side, silence."

During most of the Secret War, the lowland elites did not know that the highland villages were being bombed. American aid money flowed into the tiny Lao economy, localized around Vientiane, now artificially flush with toasters and washing machines and 24-karat gold earrings and jade bracelets, but much more money was spent on bombing the highlands only a short plane ride away. The two populations—lowlanders, wooed by American aid money, and highlanders, obliterated by American bombs—existed side by side and in ignorance of each other. This low-high division was still largely in place in Laos. Chantha had crossed the invisible border to the lowlanders when she moved to Vientiane, the only city in Laos that was never bombed. In the grand push toward development, the lowland elites had spread a narrative of revolutionary progress—the resettlement of remote villages, the Chinese plantations—that did not include this living history of war. The bombing of Laos was, and remains, a public secret carried like a canker within state-sanctioned stories of triumph: the winners of a revolution against the world's largest superpower! Laos is an authoritarian communist country without a civil society or free press: private war stories are politically taboo. Born during peacetime, Chantha was already on the other side of a border that separated the war generation from the postwar generation. On this side, ignorance.

Chantha was an absorptive presence next to me on the porch. I imagined her filling up with her aunt's memory, but with an awareness full of gaps, as a sieve slowly empties.

"Aunt, thank you for sharing your memories. People from our generation," I said and then paused, realizing that I had misspoken. I had meant to say, "people who are impacted by war," but didn't know how to say that in Lao. Chantha and Silavong were looking at me strangely. I felt Silavong's eyes wander my face, searching for signs that I had lived through what she had lived through. I had misplaced myself in the generation of grandmothers and unborns, spanning two continents, from the start of secret operations to the last active fuse—as much as three hundred years in the future, when these fuses finally decompose. Lao verbs are not conjugated, and I often lost track of time. I had used the wrong collective noun, or maybe I had spoken in the wrong tense. I tried to speak again: "We have to learn how to live out the consequences of wars that we didn't start. I was not alive to experience what you remember, but I study what happens afterward."

"It was never our war," Silavong said, waving the topic away with her hand.

After the interview, I sat on the porch and thought of the Buddhist teaching on mortality: "Existence is a burning house: get out!" And I realized that I was in that burning house still: this was

Silavong's childhood home, rebuilt on the same spot. Asking Chantha about the house, I learned that the family had rebuilt it after the war, beginning in 1975, and slowly added to it over decades until it became the largest house in the village. The new house was made with shuttered metal windows, a sturdy concrete foundation, and a tiled roof. Inflammable.

The grass house burned down, the dirt house remained, the concrete house last of all.

Silavong was an authority in the village. I accepted her collective noun—our—as forgiveness from a respected elder and a keeper of memory. Yes, this is ours: the world at war, but not our war.

Sitting safe under the house's porch eaves, I watched the rains come in the afternoon, drenching the village each day promptly at four o'clock. I enjoyed the way that the sheets of rain shook in the air like the pelt of a huge and invisible animal hung out in the wind. By five, the rains left, the road swept clean, and the chickens flocked to the pond, pecking for worms in the unsettled mud.

I told my birthday card story to Silavong who was sitting next to me on the porch. In Lao, I could talk about Christine and Cybele without using gendered pronouns—the language doesn't have male and female pronouns, and most names are gender-neutral—and I liked talking about them as just people, rather than as men or women or some other gender. I could call Christine my father without having to explain or hide her transition.

Silavong nodded, yes, that violence was common for her clients, too. A lot of people that lived through the war don't know how to stop being violent.

"It is good that your father was a monk," she said with an air of expertise, "otherwise, your family ghosts might have repeated what they experienced from the war. These injuries often repeat within families. Stopping that cycle requires spiritual work." I recognized that she was talking about PTSD, but in a way that understood trauma as a spiritual inheritance. I remembered Doctor Sawm's request and the palpable shadow of Bounmi's ghost-relative.

I didn't tell Silavong that my father was female—in Lao Buddhism, women are understood to lack the spiritual development to be monks. Men are the only monks in Laos.

"What would you have done if Cybele had come to you with their violence?"

"That's not something I can share with you. Only good Buddhists would understand the method." She waved my question off, a little sly, almost laughing at me, "But maybe I would tell your father."

4

THE CLEARANCE ZONE began at the southernmost edge of the village, where the houses abruptly stopped at the jungle frontier. The team marked the border with a red-tape cordon, left open at intervals to let people pass from one side of the village to the other and regularly staked with skull-and-crossbones signs: ANTALAI, *danger*! I passed through an opening in the cordon—and the countryside on the other side was indistinguishable. The same weatherworn stilt houses, the same vegetable gardens of eggplant and tomatoes, the same flocks of lustrous black chickens. A few dun cows roamed through the village, placidly nibbling on dry grass. The village was mostly flat grassland, nearly treeless; what forest survived the war-era defoliating agents had since been illegally sold for lumber across the Vietnam border. As a result, the village was moderately well-off, but denuded, a town of tree stumps. The jungle to the south was an anomaly saved from the lumber trade by the lingering cluster strike. I could see where the strike began by looking to the red cordon, but before the clearance team came, this older tree line marked where the villagers had found the border by trial and error with their machetes.

This village had been part of the Ho Chi Minh Trail, the infamous military supply route between Laos and Vietnam during the war. The old trail could still be recognized by seismic traces, like the activity above an underground fault line: war scrap traders prowled these paths for their next claim; shrines to dead travelers crowded together in places, regular as roadside markers; there were patches of recently cleared land pockmarked with fresh demolition craters; hulks of old machinery, alien and unidentifiable; and areas locals had abandoned, deemed unlucky and left to the cows, wide pastures where live bombs lingered. The state and its development partners renovated parts of the trail into paved and painted roads, cleared of bombs, cleared of shrines, but it was as if these new roads were set apart from the surrounding land by their novelty. So far, the clearance team working this village had found two hundred items of ordnance over about seventy-eight square meters cleared, almost all cluster submunitions.

I walked a dirt track running south to north through the village and mused that it might have been part of that supply route fifty years ago. The track ended at a large wooden stilt house with a spacious understory. The team was headquartered at the house of the chief, the largest house in the village. Only clearance technicians— searchers, demolition specialists, the team leader, and the field manager—were in this part of the village today. In preparation for the demolition, the team had temporarily evacuated all of the residents. One of the searchers was on permanent duty to keep the cows out of the clearance zone.

Moving toward the house in the bare heat of the open fields, I felt beads of sweat rolling down my back. It hadn't rained in months— this was good for clearance since the bombs stayed put.

In the cool shade beneath the chief's house, Channarong gestured me over with a wave.

"Here, these are yours," he said and handed me a large blue duffle bag with my assigned safety gear. I took the gear out of its duffle, carefully examining each piece in turn: a blue high-impact plastic visor with a clear face shield wrapped in felt; a set of leather gloves; and a bulky blue Kevlar vest with a front flap, neatly folded into a rectangle. This was the first time that I had encountered this kind of safety gear at a clearance site.

"Can you help me put this on correctly?" I asked half-joking, turning to Channarong, who was unpacking his duffel on the ground next to me.

"Sure."

I unfolded the Kevlar vest and held it up to my body. Seeing that the vest only covered my abdomen, I startled: "This is no protection for cowards!"

"You're a safe rectangle; no arms and legs," Channarong chuckled while carefully positioning the vest over my shoulders. Immediately, I felt the unexpected weight of the Kevlar plate dragging my shoulders down. I moved my body experimentally, twisting, comparing the free movement of my unprotected arms with the constrained motion of my protected torso. The material of the vest was stiff, unwieldy. And the front flap made it difficult to move my legs. The day was hot, and I could already feel the vest heating up and making my shirt soggy. Continuing my explorations, I found a convenient little pocket on the front of the vest into which I put my field notebook, pencil, and camera.

Channarong instructed me in the proper body positions for maximizing the protection of the vest and visor in the event of an accidental explosion. The gear protected the wearer against the direct explosion of a landmine, assuming the wearer was defusing the mine and thus facing directly into the blast. To demonstrate, he knelt in the dirt, his hands on the ground pantomiming that he was digging up a mine.

"The idea is that if you kneel like this over the item, then the vest and helmet will create a seam that protects you from knee to the top of your head."

He bent his head down until the bottom of the visor was flush against the breastplate of the vest, and then traced the seam with his finger. The bottom flap of the Kevlar vest partially covered his thighs and knees. His arms and hands were unprotected—bomb techs needed nimble fingers. In the event of a landmine exploding, his body from knees to head, the width of the vest, would be comparatively protected.

"This is only true in the case of a landmine explosion," he explained. Cluster munitions, the most common type of ordnance in Laos, explode at a different speed and generally fragment. The Kevlar vest and visor would only limit the penetration of these fragments, without mitigating their deadliness. There are no international standards, and no standardized safety gear, for cluster munition clearance. Laos is unique in being predominantly cluster bombed and has more of this type of bomb per capita than any other country in the world. As a result of the country's extremely high rates of cluster munition contamination—and a recent global shift in war-making toward cluster munitions, drone strikes, and other forms of air warfare—Laos was gaining importance as an international laboratory for cluster munition clearance. Global clearance practices were out of step with the risks of air warfare. Channarong hoped to develop better methods and specialized equipment for clearing these types of ordnance.

"But for now," Channarong said to me with a laugh sharp and short, "our safety gear is mostly for show."

I laughed with him, hiding my uncertainty. In my field research so far, I had spent more time with survey teams than demolition teams. I thought about the demolition pit out in the jungle, beyond the border of the village, a hole in the ground lined with the dark spheres of cluster munitions stacked like fruit in a farmer's cellar. Every other clearance operator I worked with went without specialized safety gear, partially because no specialized gear was available, partially because of the risk of sunstroke when wearing insulated clothing in the tropics. This was my first time working with Channarong's demolition team, and I had not yet been out to see them in action. I imagined walking toward that explosion later in the day, after lunch, knowing that my safety gear was "mostly for show." I wondered which would feel safer: having no safety gear, or having the wrong kind?

The fields surrounding the stilt house crackled in the dry season winds. We stood in the shade of the house's understory, waiting on lunch and for the team to return from preparing the planned demolition site. At last, a group of five bomb techs walked single file down a slim dirt path through the field toward us. They wore identical dark blue uniforms; their blue visors tipped up like crowns above their heads. Their blue solemnity was indelible against the noonday yellow of the fields—I had the sense of a vision appearing, simmering in the heat. Each was holding a bundle of grains upright in front of them, heads bowed, nibbling on the stalks. It was common for bomb techs to forage for wild foods from the area surrounding clearance sites. They progressed toward us like a row of supplicants, presenting their offerings. I accepted a stalk from one of them, though I could not identify the plant. The grains were like tiny round pearls, slightly green, dangling on slender threads around a single central stalk. Using our teeth, we nipped the grains off the threads and broke them open, with a delightfully audible popping sound, in our mouths.

Their equipment (the metal detectors, buckets, hand-shovels, rope, and colored stakes) was left mostly at the demolition site. But a pile of leather gloves, vests, and helmets was growing on the divan like an offering, something precious given away. I added my safety gear to the pile.

One of the other searchers produced a pink plastic bag of bitter greens she had foraged during her breaks in clearance. Pennywort whose leaves are half-moons; shiny dark green lozenges of pepper leaf; and the thin blades of jasmine shoots, crushed and releasing their fragrance like perfume. The searchers spread lunch out on the wooden divan in the shade of the stilt house: there were sauces made of roasted garlic, eggplant, and peppers. And a giant bamboo basket of sticky rice cooked by the villagers for the team, which we scooped out with our hands and used to sop up the thick, spicy condiments. Sun-dried pork jerky, called sien savanh, *heavenly meat,* preserved with sugar and chilies and flecked with sesame seeds, was delicious torn off and chewed in thick chunks. That morning, I had purchased a whole fish, speared and fire-roasted on lemongrass stalks, and wrapped in sheets of oiled banana leaves, to bring as my lunch contribution. Under the silver-scaled skin, which we peeled back like a folio, the white flesh of the fish broke into crescent sheets sturdy enough to pick up with our fingers. The bitter herbs were a surprising palliative, cool water in the heat. We sat on our heels in the dirt, eating with our hands like contented chickens pecking in a garden full of corn and fat beetles.

Conversation meandered through the active clearance sites in the area, offering updates on other field teams. I listened, less sure of my Lao skills, but did manage to slip in a few questions.

"What makes this demolition different from the others you've done?" I asked Dao, a demolition specialist sitting next to me.

"It's the same. They're all the same. If a demolition is different, we know we're doing it wrong, and it will be unsafe. We have to stick with procedure, which is very strict. You'll see when we dem them after lunch." She said dem, short for the English word *demolition.*

I nodded. "Are you the one setting up the dem?"

She nodded proudly. "Yes, I'm better at deming than at searching. I'm the one pressing the trigger."

"I'm surprised that we have safety gear, especially since it's not specialized for this type of demolition." I gestured to the pile of vests and visors on the divan.

"Yes, I know what you mean." She thought for a moment with one finger delicately on her chin. "It makes me feel better to know that I have it, even if it's not designed for this kind of bomb. I think people feel safer when they have safety gear, even though we know that real safety comes from proper procedures, not gear."

"How do procedures keep you safer?"

"Well, for example, we've picked a good safe point." The safe point was a spot just outside the predicted blast radius, measured to the meter on the ground, where the team met to supervise the dem. "Our safe point is far away from the pit but not yet in the ban. This is a tough site because the houses are so close to the bomb point." The bomb point was the center of the blast radius, the pit where the bombs were buried and sandbagged in preparation for being blown up. "As long as everyone comes out of the forest and joins me at the safe point, we'll be fine."

Then she turned to me, "Your lemongrass fish was perfect. What do you think of Lao food?"

I smiled appreciatively. I thought about the country's present history of starvation: famine struck shortly after the war, and the new state was forced to abandon its efforts at collective farming. That was well within the lifetime of the older techs. It was an act of care to ask someone about their food.

"I think the food is delicious." I patted my stomach. "Sep teh sep vaa!" *This is really delicious!*

On my other side, an older bomb tech clapped delightedly and passed a plate of spicy eggplant, saying, "Eat more please!"

Our feasting was cut short by Syha, the team leader, who stood up without saying a word. The signal that lunch was over. Syha was a middle-aged, thin man with a permanently stoic expression and an oval face; his skin pulled taut without a trace of fat, framed by chin-length black hair. There were rumors about him—that he had fought as a revolutionary, which he neither confirmed nor denied.

The sticky rice was still steaming when the searchers replaced its bamboo cover. Following the lead of another technician, I gathered what remained of the food and threw it to the nearest flock of chickens, adding to a little pile of bones and peels of fruit forming at the edge of the understory. I cleaned my hands at a neighbor's small spigot of freshwater, one of the few water sources in the village, but without soap I couldn't remove the lemongrass smell.

When I returned to collect my safety gear from the communal pile, a team medic was waiting for me with her clipboard. Two medics were permanently stationed at this house, far beyond the precisely calculated radius of the demolition. Their movements through the clearance zone were controlled; they were only allowed to enter the zone one at a time to prevent a scenario where both died and left the team without a medic.

"Please sign in," she said and handed me her clipboard of columns. Time In: 11:30 a.m.; Reason for Visit: Research; Blood Type: B–.

I handed the clipboard back to her. The medic glanced down and then said cheerily, "You are lucky! We always have that blood available. It's a common blood type in Laos." And she pointed matter-of-factly to an insulated foam case where she stored the blood.

I stared at this case for a moment, my mind blank, until Dao caught my attention with a tap on my elbow: "Here—take these in your pocket to snack on later!" and handed me a few tan globes of longan. Food can be a language of care.

"Thank you! That is kind," I replied. Each "dragon eye" fruit was small, nearly round, a white viscous pulp surrounding a hard, smooth black nut looking remarkably like a clouded eye. They were eaten by forcefully pressing the tips of one's thumbs into the thin tan shell until it cracked open, two lids parting to reveal the soft flesh.

I caught Channarong smiling when he saw me slip Dao's fruit into my vest's front pocket. A little further down the dirt path past the chief's house, the path toward the demolition site, he told me, "They like you—because you eat with them and you speak Lao."

"You eat with them, too."

"Yeah, but not the sour green stuff," he said, scrunching his nose, referring to the foraged herbs. "I like food that's from grocery stores."

I thought I knew what grocery stores he was talking about in his upscale Bangkok neighborhood: sprawling, maze-like warrens of chilly indoor shops. Vegetables individually wrapped in crinkling plastic pouches. A hundred types of purple taro bread, fluffy and light as cartoon food.

The sky was untarnished and without clouds. There was no wind, and the only sound was the faint clinking of wooden bells far off, bells which the farmers hung around the necks of their water buffalo. We made our way toward the clearance site at the edge of the village. It was a trash zone; the villagers chose not to cultivate it because they knew that it was heavily contaminated.

Through the trees, I saw more skull-and-crossbones signs announcing the site before I could see any of the techs. As we moved further into the jungle, I noticed a cable snaking through the underbrush. Clean line, drawn carefully in a vibrant sunflower yellow. Meant to be seen. It was mostly straight, without any kinks, and bent gracefully around the thick roots of the trees.

Pointing at the cable, I asked, "What is this?"

With glinting eyes, enjoying his expertise: "You'll see soon. Let's keep walking." Then he placed a hand on my shoulder, gently steering me behind him. "Past this point, don't walk in front of me."

At the team meeting that morning, Syha concluded his briefing by reminding his team of their five core safety rules. He held up his hand and pointed at each of his fingers in turn, saying: "One: Always follow in the steps of a senior team member; Two: Never walk off the paths; Three: No chatting in the clearance zone; Four: Don't touch anything metal without permission; Five: If there is an unplanned explosion, wait at the safe point and follow my instructions." Then he closed his fist above his head, in a gesture that reminded me of a military salute. Per protocol, Syha gave his team these five-fingered reminders at every morning briefing. Channarong was reminding me of Rule Number One ("Always follow in the steps of a senior team member").

Channarong and I tracked the yellow cable into the jungle. Some of the bigger, bushier plants were macheted out of the way, making a kind of tunnel for the cable. Then, a few further meters in, the trees were savaged, roughly hacked, underbrush stacked in fresh, sap-green smelling piles. The team had cut the trees and scrub to make room for their work. Now the hot, bright sunlight warmed me inside my safety gear. Glare got into my eyes, and I tripped over a mangled tree root.

Channarong reached out to catch my arm. He lowered his voice, all concern: "Are you afraid? We don't have to go any further." "No, I'm fine. This isn't my first demolition. I just tripped." I untangled my legs, smoothed down the lower flap of the Kevlar vest. I didn't think I was afraid of the demolition, but as I was falling forward, I had a vision of myself tripping over a bomb and blowing us both up. "Thank you for checking."

A few steps on, I added: "I looked up the actuary rates for explosives clearance, did I ever tell you? You know, the injury rates that insurance companies use to figure out how much they're going to charge you for insurance. Being a professional ping-pong player was considered riskier than being a bomb technician."

"Is that true?"

"Apparently actuaries think so!"

He thought for a moment. "Makes sense. I sometimes think that the safest place to be in Laos is at the clearance site: that's where the medics are and all the safety equipment. We map and mark the bombs. Whereas, in the rest of Laos, nobody knows where the bombs are."

Then he stopped in the middle of the path, set his hands on his hips, and laughed. Surprised, I almost ran into him.

"Also, of course, our injury rates are low!" he announced. "If there's an accident, you'll just die! No injuries, no medical expenses. Probably very cheap."

And then, after we continued a little bit further down the path: "Glad I'm not a ping-pong player."

We followed the cable to where it terminated at a small pit, carefully surrounded by red stakes. This was the bomb point, the center of the demolition.

The searchers had carefully scooped out the soil with their bare hands and small spades. It was necessary to be very careful when moving the soil surrounding buried bombs. At the bottom of the shallow pit, I saw several half-submerged BLU-26, a spherical cluster submunition distinguished by a fluted spiral pattern around the clamp ring that joins the bomb's hemispheres. American weapons manufacturers embedded the casing with hundreds of pieces of fragments designed to maim, rather than kill, as many people as possible within the blast radius. In Laos, BLU-26 were colloquially known as "guava bombs" for their resemblance to the khaki colored, spherical fruit. The ordnance in the pit were painted dusty green, bleeding rosettes of orange rust where the original paint was flaking. They looked almost moldy like they might crumble if I touched one even very gently. In the afternoon's planned demolition, these bombs would finally detonate a half-century after being dropped in the war.

Syha moved aside so that I could get in closer to the pit.

"Don't touch. Have you seen this kind of ordnance before?" he asked softly in Lao. As he spoke, Syha glanced at Channarong, who was standing just out of earshot. Channarong understood Lao well, but he only spoke to his team in English. Lao was the language of the poor, he said. This meant that Channarong's team was quicker to finish their reports, which were all in English anyway. But it also added an extra pressure to perform, particularly for the searchers who didn't speak English fluently. There was more translation work for the multilingual team members.

"Yes," I said. "I'm familiar with this type."

I knelt over the half-buried bombs, remembering to tuck my chin down so that the seam of my faceplate was flush with my Kevlar vest, as Channarong had taught me. A distracted thought: we are all wearing the wrong safety gear.

"Syha, will you describe to me what I am looking at?"

The team leader gestured for me to stand up next to him, a half-meter away from the pit; searchers were working nearby, and Rule Number Three ("No chatting in the clearance zone") was meant to keep down distractions. Clearance sites were quiet places until something exploded.

Syha spoke to me formally: "I selected the BLU-26 pit for a demolition site based on its distance from the ban, its relation to nearby tree and soil features that would deflect the blast, and the soil composition. All the ordnance in this area are the same type, BLU-26, which are safe to destroy in a shared pit." He indicated the demolition pit with a pointed finger, where a group of searchers were filling sandbags. "I am having some of the searchers surround the bomb point with sandbags, as a training exercise. Some of them have never done this before." He shrugged, glancing at me, "It is very routine; I know my team can do it."

I gestured to the clearing full of holes. "Do you teach people how to dig holes in training?"

"Yes, we do!" A rare smile. "Very carefully, without pressure. If the soil is very hard, you are allowed to step on the blade very softly. It is important to not press too hard like you would with a shovel." He pantomimed using a foot to press a shovel's blade into the soil. "It is necessary to use this small kind of shovel—a spade—to make the holes."

Syha pulled his spade off a belt loop. Handmade, the blade short and still black from the forge where the color hadn't been polished off with use. He had carved the handle from a knobby tree branch. "Once you've uncovered the item, it is better to dig the rest with your hands."

There were no bird songs—they hunted songbirds—but the searchers filled the clearing with the repeated small thud and scrape of spades moving soil very slowly. Syha pointed again, drawing my attention to a technician working a few meters away from us: she was on her knees, lifting another BLU-26 out of its hole. She held the bomb in her cupped hands, softly, a little out in front of her, never taking her eyes off of it—I have seen nothing else held with that charged combination of patience and danger. She transferred the bomb into a blue bucket padded with a sandbag and carried the bucket to the pit. She was carefully, gently carrying in her bucket each of the ordnance found in the clearing to the pit, one at a time. Not all cluster submunitions could be moved in this manner—some of them had delayed fuses that were triggered by even the subtle movement of being lifted.

Next to the pit, Channarong was hovering over three techs packing sandbags. He towered over them, at least a foot taller. He lifted a bag theatrically and said in a loud military voice, "Does this feel like twenty kilos to you? It needs to be twenty-five!"

The three searchers cringed a little and redoubled their shovel work. I couldn't tell how they took his badgering—Channarong could be very intimidating when he wanted to be. As the most senior technician, it was understood that he could speak as loud as he wanted even as everyone else was silent as mice. Having delivered his instructions at booming volume, Channarong then made his way back over to me.

Pointing at the yellow cable, I whispered, "Hey, I still don't know what that wire is."

"Okay, let's go check it out."

With a final shouted reminder to keep track of the sandbag weight, Channarong then gestured for me to follow him out of the clearing. The sunflower-yellow line slithered back into the refreshing shade of the trees not yet cut down.

"You know, normally guests aren't allowed to get within twenty-five meters of active clearance. The searchers are supposed to stop and wait for the guest to move further away."

"Is it okay that they let me get close?"

"I'm going to talk to them about it later . . . but you are with me, so it's different. You are not a guest; you are *my* guest." He wiggled his eyebrows at me, making me laugh. He was an internationally recognized expert in cluster munitions clearance—being "his" guest gave me greater access as a researcher. But earning greater access to this field site came with specific dangers. As I moved closer to my research subjects, I was also moving closer to the center of an explosion. How close did I want to get? What was the proper distance for researching explosives?

After a few more steps, he continued: "It's a safety thing. It has to do with how much risk you are in—which is also our legal liability. Twenty-five meters is the required safety distance for guests. Ten meters is the required safety distance for searchers. Nine meters is the blast radius for a BLU-26."

"So, how much risk was I in, getting that close?"

"Right next to that pile of BLU-26? If it had gone off, you would have died instantly. But it is improbable that it would go off, just like that, without anyone moving it."

"What about at ten meters?"

"You'd be okay. Ten meters is survival with injuries. At ten meters, we'd be hit with fragments, probably lose an arm or our legs, but we'd survive."

"Ah, a safe rectangle!"

"Yup."

We crossed the border of the jungle and reentered the village, keeping to our side of the cordon. At the periphery of the village, the cable terminated in a large spool half unwound and looking out of scale, like a bobbin of thread strangely enlarged. Next to it, Dao was unpacking equipment from a plastic case—the demolition trigger mechanism. And not far away, on the other side of the cordon, a group of village women were sitting on their porch watching the clearance preparations. The women, a mixed group of young and old, provided friendly commentary on the team's activities, gossiping, and teasingly offering to share their whiskey. Dao smiled when she saw us approaching.

"It's the trigger wire," Channarong declared proudly. "That's how we'll control the dem from a safe distance."

Prompted by an animated voice from her radio, Dao leaned forward to pick up the yellow cable. Her movements were unsteady, and she used her hands to align her left leg as she bent her knees. When she bent over, the hem of her pants legs rose above the line of her boots. Surprised, I noticed at the demolition what I had not seen at lunch—that her left leg was prosthetic. The material of her leg was white, almost translucent like bone. It was a model I was familiar with from other clearance sites—these white plastic "work legs" were specially manufactured for searchers. The legs had no metal parts and did not interfere with the use of metal detectors.

Before I can properly think about Dao's work leg, I have a sudden sense of time speeding up, or counting down. The doors between the trees open, branches bending aside; bomb techs emerge from the jungle in twos and threes, all at once, forming an advancing line of blue uniforms. Aroused like a flock of birds, radios are chattering, fizzing static phrases—who is here? Is everyone safe? I also hear laughter, shouts of excitement. Syha raises his hand, wordless, and there is silence.

Dao is holding a small box with both her hands—I see a comically large, bright red round button. Other techs gather around her; I move in. Someone is leaning against my arm, but I cannot tell if it is an embrace or a gentle push away. Like a flock of angels on the head of a pin: in this moment, the safe point feels without limit, an expanding promise of shelter where we each might fit without encumbrance. My roots are going down deep, pushing through damp earth and dry rivers, through the fault lines lifting these mountains into the skies, through veins of silver that draw the lightening to ground. I am becoming all nerves. I do not know if I am breathing, but I feel alive. Each sensation is coming to me as if through all of our bodies at once. Near, I feel the soft rush of taking and holding breath.

Syha declares each syllable slowly, precisely:
"One ... two ... three ... go!"

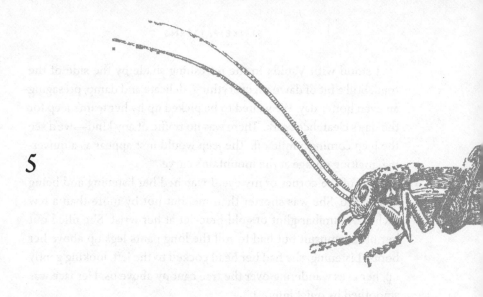

5

THE HEAT, lazy as a cloud of flies, hovered over us. The heat was humming, the cicadas seeming to vibrate the air. Their warm buzz would crescendo until deafening and then recede to near silence, only to start up again. Vanida and I could only talk in the pauses between bug songs when the air seemed to quiet like the surface of a still pond. Their songs were everywhere, and I listened with my whole body rather than just with my ears. There was nothing to do but listen, it was too hot; I tried to distinguish the sounds of different insects, though I often couldn't name what species I was hearing: the familiar cicada chorus; a vibrato tenor, perhaps a large cricket; then a lazy drone that lifted and dropped like melody; a swooning tremolo soloist; and a percussion of jittery tap-taps of unfathomable origin.

At the next pause, Vanida said, "You know, they are listening to us."

"Who?"

"The bugs. They take turns talking and listening; and right now, they are listening to us."

We were both silent, curious, and sure enough, the bugs started up again.

I stood with Vanida in the refreshing shade by the side of the road. Still a bit of dawn on everything, delicate and damp, presaging an even hotter day. We waited to be picked up by her team's jeep for the day's clearance work. There was no traffic of any kind—we'd see the jeep coming a mile off. The jeep would first appear as a quivering, melting mirage at the mountain's curve.

Out of the corner of my eye, I watched her listening and being listened to. She was shorter than me, but not by more than a few inches. A familiar glint of gold bracelet at her wrist. She filled out her blue jumpsuit but had to roll the long pants legs up above her boots. Listening, she had her head cocked to the left, looking gently up, her eyes wandering over the tree canopy above us. Her face was smoothed by quiet interest.

We live with so many beings that we do not understand. The bug voices—not really voices, more like vibrations made by their bodies—were mostly incomprehensible to me. I knew they were sending messages to each other, but I didn't know what bugs talked about beyond things like sex and death. Many species speak with words for which my native language has no translation. Without an interpreter, the effort of understanding was sometimes nearly unsurmountable. Being with these others makes it necessary to dwell in not knowing. At the horizon, the world turned mirage: a mix of strange and familiar, the familiar made strange by distance. What do bugs say, what do bugs hear? Vanida and I and the bugs, we took turns listening to each other.

I felt the familiar prick of a mosquito on my forearm. Without a thought, I slapped it: raising my palm flat in front of us, I saw a small red-brown smudge, my own blood coloring mangled wings. And then immediately felt a rush of regret for the tiny loss of insect life.

Vanida looked down at the smudge and then up at me, surprised: "You just killed it!"

Her face moved from surprise to sadness, and then to disappointment.

Only the most devout swatted off mosquitoes instead of killing them. I half-apologized, "I'm not a Buddhist, Vanida."

The guest house was a converted French villa, probably built for a colonial administrator and then abandoned during the First Indochina War when France began to cede control of its colonies. The remains of a rose garden slumped in the yard, faint pathways visible under the vines. At the edges of the garden, the forest was a wall of faded green spotted with red hibiscus, home of the orchestra of insects. In the middle of the garden was the two-story villa whose walls of clay bousillage soaked up sunlight like dew. Four doors, one on each side, were painted a deep unctuous red. Inside, the guest house was still laid out like a villa, without a front desk or room numbers on the doors, but everything had been painted over in white. There was tap water, unreliable. There were also white towels and white sheets, and a span of white tiled floors. I assumed we were staying here because this was the only guest house in the area. The place didn't have a name—the housekeeper, who lived across the street, called it the "clearance hotel" because the only folks that stayed there were explosives clearance staffers and American soldiers on POW missions. The reading material I found in the common room was a ten-month old copy of *Stars and Stripes*, the American military periodical.

If the villa was abandoned during the First Indochina War, that would have been around 1946, when anti-colonial movements against French rule escalated into armed conflict. Laos had been part of French Indochina, the territory that is now the independent states of Vietnam, Laos, and Cambodia. In Vietnam, the war for independence was sparked by Ho Chi Minh's declaration of the Democratic Republic of Vietnam in 1945; subsequently, a series of failed talks dissolved into guerrilla warfare and fragile international diplomacy. The United States backed the French and their colonies, preferring puppet monarchies to communist republics. But these same cultural and political shifts were also occurring in France, and the French liberal and communist elite were gaining political power; under pressure from its own citizens, France eventually withdrew its colonial administrators and military support for Indochina. The United States continued to arm the conflict—alongside the Soviet Union, China, Japan, and other Cold War constituents—and the Indochina War gradually escalated into the Vietnam-American War and then the Secret War in Laos. For many in Laos, the communist revolution of 1975 was the latest in a decades-long struggle for independence from a succession of armed imperial powers.

At the villa, the insects were the true regular guests, and they freely slipped from room to room, humming wild love songs. Though the villa was huge, and we were the only guests, Vanida and I would be sharing a single bedroom with two twin beds. My first night there alone, I discovered that the room already hosted a mysterious nighttime creature that was slowly chewing its way out through the ceiling in the corner—or perhaps it was chewing its way in? Confident that I wasn't its prey, its methodical munching lulled me to sleep. Each morning, I inspected the hole. I tracked the expansion of the toothed, rounded edges, but the shape was too irregular to give me any clues about the creature's physical properties. There was almost no debris on the floor of our room, so I suspected that it ate its progress. Above was only black: the windowless space under the peaked, tiled roof. I noticed the hole was gnawed slightly larger every day, but I never saw the creature. The white tiles glared, glossy and oblivious.

On that first night by myself, I also noticed that there was something munching its way through my pillow: I could hear it when I slept on my side, with my ear pressed to the white pillowcase. I could smell the bleach in the sheets. The whiteness everywhere took on a sinister quality, like a sheet thrown over a mirror in a house of mourning. Increasingly unsure of what I might see beneath the whiteness, I rolled one of my shirts into a headrest. At night, I still heard the munching through my makeshift pillow—a phantom sound.

I had arrived a day before Vanida and the rest of the team, intending to scope out the town. To get around, I planned on asking a local driver to take me to the clearance headquarters on the edge of town. I wanted to introduce myself to the local staff before arranging to be picked up later with Vanida from the guest house. Alerted that there was a person staying at the old villa, that morning there was already a driver slumbering in his seat just beyond the gate, staking out his fare. I was the only lodger. Though I had never seen this man before in my life, I knew he could only be waiting for me. I gently tapped on the hood of his three-wheeled taxi, called a tuk-tuk.

"Sabaidee! How are you this morning?"

He trundled awake, gurgling like an old engine, bleary-eyed. His tuk-tuk was three-fourths wood, a weathered frame for passengers laid on top of an antique motorcycle, much like a sidecar, the whole vehicle wrapped in salvaged plastic advertising banners. On one banner, a young woman with sparkling white teeth held a slim bottle of toothpaste above the marketing phrase HAVE GOOD CIVILIZA-TION. I silently traced the Thai word, sivilai for *civilization*, on the roof of my mouth. White teeth, emblem of modern luxury. Through the mouth comes the world, out of the mouth comes the word.

"Sabaidee . . . your Lao is pretty good!" He chuckled, rubbed his eyes, and grabbed a rumpled tweed cap hanging on the handle of his motorcycle. Manchester United stickers puckered the metal chassis and wrinkled like skin in the sun. The hat firmly on his head, he turned to me now fully awake. We smiled at each other.

I pulled out Channarong's business card and showed him the logo of the organization, thinking that he might recognize it. There were no addresses or street names in town, and I had never been to the clearance headquarters before. I started trying to explain: "I want to go to the bomb organization . . . where they blow up bombs."

"Oh, you want to go BOOM?" he said, pitching his arms out like an expanding debris cloud.

I hesitated a moment and then said, "Yes, I want to go boom."

"Okay, I will take you there. They have lots of bombs."

The price of the ride was reasonable—but I worried that I was going to get more than I bargained for.

On another morning, Vanida and I agreed to go to the market before her shift started, and after I would take our groceries home by myself. She would head off to the clearance site, and I would go back to the villa to type up my notes and interviews.

I set my alarm for five, before the market opened, so as to arrive for the small and bright hours before the day got too hot. No one was going to sit out in the sun with their wilting produce past seven, Vanida warned me. Her clearance team kept similar hours: starting at six, breaking for the hottest part of the day, and doing paperwork indoors for the afternoon.

Making coffee for the two of us in the attached outdoor kitchen, I let the early morning smell wake me up. My senses started to sharpen, but were still unfocused, and I noticed the scuff of red dirt on the tiles without at first recognizing my own tracks. For a half-moment, I wondered about my large-jawed nighttime lodger: I wondered if its tracks might look like mine. What might its feet look like? Did it have feet?

Outside, the world was swaddled in a thick mist, suffused with a light cut into bars by the trees and buildings. Stark slices of air, a shadow architecture. It was hard to see what was in the shadows lying like night beneath the trees—looking at the garden, I had a paper-cut sense of sharp outlines glued together. I handed Vanida her coffee in a travel mug, and we headed to the market.

The mist was cloying, thick, and softly glowing a melted-butter yellow. I felt that we were walking through a clinging substance, like fluffs of spiderweb, that needed to be sliced open to make our path. We were inside a cloud moored on the mountain crag. We turned out the gate and started walking the road, which sloped gently upwards, hugging the ridge. The trees were dark and slightly rustling. We smelled the musk of wet earth and the fragrant crush of leaves pressed by the heavy mist. A vista opened to our right. Like a curtain lifted, we saw the valley illuminated from the low horizon, high-relief and long shadows. The lands below were nearly burnt, long swaths of bare farmland razed with sunlight. A procession of karst cliffs puzzled perspective, some topped with small forests. Wisps of cloud warmed into curls beyond the cliffs that progressed away from us in shades of magenta. The light was of such thickness that it carved the karst, lengthened and lifted as if giants' teeth pulled up from the valley floor.

Where the road ran along the peak of the mountain, the houses fell away to either side, as if floating in air. Built on stilts, neighboring homes were sometimes several meters different in elevation, suspended above each other. These homes were taller than the mountains themselves. The ground seemed to disappear, and it was easy to imagine flying off into the mists.

The market was in a flattened area bordering a precipice above the villages of the valley below. We walked into the view: the road ended at the edge, and we could go no further. I felt the cliff at the corner of my sight; I was not used to living in these elevations. The market leaned against the nothing-air, nearer to the edge then I would go—so near, I thought that if I looked over the side, I might see a few shops rigged to the rock. Vendors had set up awnings, some cut fresh from nearby vegetation, and patched plastic tents were staked to the ground, lest they fly away like kites. Many more had no awnings and sat on folded woven mats or tarps, their goods laid before them in neatly ordered piles, the pale sky behind. Perhaps I have spent too much of my life in houses: I had the sense of walking from a small room into a huge empty space, roofless, whose walls and floor might fall away at any moment.

There was a smell of fresh pepper, spicy and crushed underfoot. I thought that it was the smell of the upper air—the smell of a cliff's edge, bird's heights, and the pillars of karst.

Vanida exchanged friendly chatter with the vendors. I overheard that several had trekked their goods from above this village, at the very spine of the mountains, and had been walking for hours already before the dawn. There were mostly woman selling and mostly women buying: from the villages of the valley floor, Lao woman in sihns and scarves; from higher up the mountain, Ahka woman in pleated black turbans decorated with strips of brightly colored homespun hung with silver coins, mostly French coins, but increasingly also Chinese and Taiwanese currency. Some women's hats were sewn thick as chainmail with silver: coins, flowers, balls, and tinkling bells. On the French coins: *République Française* printed around an image of Marianne, the female embodiment of the Republic, sitting in splendor on her silver throne, crowned with a glowing diadem. On other coins, her face was in profile, proud and unsmiling, wearing her Phrygian cap. 1907, 1910, 1926. I noticed a few American half-dollars, but no smaller change, each large coin sewn in a place of importance at the center-front or center-back of the women's hats. 1955, 1962, coins from the American-funded insurgency. Though the women prized coins from global trade, as far afield as America or Mexico, this market was as far as they would go; some of these women had never set foot on the valley floor.

Each woman sold a small selection, no more than a half-dozen items, so it was necessary to buy from many women to complete our grocery list: several types of chili, white sesame seeds, garlic, green baby eggplant, long beans, limes, mint and local herbs, crickets, and sticky rice. Incense for prayer.

My ear was caught by a loud, slick chopping. Each time I heard the chop, I shook a little, as if threatened by a knife. A quick look found the source of the sound: a pineapple seller with a machete and a wooden block. I was hearing the cry of her chopping block. Her entire body flexed, arm held high, and then rammed down as she hacked the honeycomb skin from the fruit and the leaves from the stalk. Lined up for sale, the prepared pineapples looked like skinned heads on sticks. Flies buzzed around her block and supped at the sticky ooze.

"In Lao, we say that pineapples have eyes," Vanida said, noticing my interest. The fruit's skin did look a bit like compound insect eyes.

"Do they watch us?" I asked.

"The pineapples aren't the ones that are watching us," she said through a cryptic smile and turned away from me, walking farther into the market. I followed.

At another stall, Vanida ran her fingers through a basket of short-grain white rice. Luxurious: the sound of the grains pattering each other as they fell.

"This mountain rice is special," she explained to me. "More flavorful because they can only do one harvest a year up here and use less water—in the valley, we do two or more harvests, so our rice is less intensely flavored. You will taste the difference."

We stopped in front of an older woman selling insects, still alive and wriggling in their baskets. Giant cockroaches in a plastic bowl, the sides too deep and slippery for them to climb out of, too innocent to know to fly away. Their carapaces were delicate as folded wax paper. Next to the fully-grown cockroaches, a basket of white grubs squeezed themselves together like fat fingers in a fist.

The Lao Buddhists of the valley believe that we don't live one life. We have many, many lives that we move through, one to the next, hopefully improving ourselves with each new breath. Rarely are we reincarnated as people—that requires a lot of spiritual development—but more often, we are animals. If we reincarnate as insects, we're the lowest of the low, and our lives are very short. Swatted by a wet palm, squashed under heel, we move on quickly. Life as a bug is a lesson in mortality. Lao Buddhists believe that those of us reincarnated as humans are fortunate, for humans are capable of enlightenment. We that exist are everything that came before: all the mothers and fathers, animal and humans, kin and kind. And after this life, we will become new beings, daughters of different fathers. Each of us, in a faraway past life, has almost certainly been a beetle.

I pointed at the large, pulsing grubs. "What about these?"

Vanida shook her head. "Oh no, those aren't any good. The big ones are bitter." And then she leaned on my arm and whispered in

English so that the women would not understand us, "Only the poor eat those."

She picked up a funnel-shaped basket of crickets and shook it to judge their jump. To the woman, she said in Lao, "This is not very fresh." And then to me, in English, "We could get these for a stir-fry." Vanida only killed or ate animals for food and never in sport or defense, as I had slapped the mosquito.

Vanida agreed on a price for the crickets—the woman gave us the basket on loan so that I could carry them home.

Crickets must be cooked carefully to prevent them from jumping away. I put the whole basket in the refrigerator and left them long enough to freeze. Vanida advised me that if the fridge wasn't cold enough, I was to drown them in their basket. The fridge was enough. And that evening, I shook their cold shrunken bodies out into a colander, washed them, and then fried them with lime leaves, chilies, and garlic. Delicate parts, like their antennae and front legs, quickly burned and broke off to make a kind of powdery sauce. Their smell was like fried fresh butter, creamy and herbaceous. Their taste and texture was like fried chicken skin, crunchy and oiled. Satisfied, the two of us had full stomachs. I kept the basket as the old woman had made me promise to bring it back to her. The funnel-shaped basket was also a trap: the crickets climbed in through the opening, and then couldn't remember how to get out. The old woman emptied the trap and then reset it until filled; emptied and filled, emptied and filled.

I told Vanida that there was a strange pattern on the wood of the door to our hotel bedroom. When I first saw it, I thought—it was a face! Wood whorls, tight as a fingerprint.

I pointed the shape out to her. It was on the back of the bedroom door, visible from the beds if we had the door closed.

"Does this look like a face to you?"

She looked at me, no expression, and didn't look at the door.

"I think it's a face," I repeated, assuming she hadn't understood.

She was still silent, almost ignoring me.

"What is it, Vanida?"

"Come on, I'll tell you outside."

She hesitated at the back door, then turned and grabbed a package of incense, and went out. I followed her to the outdoor kitchen and not the rose garden. All around us was the thick sound of early evening crickets. Felt-winged moths flapped shadows around the kitchen's single bulb.

I was a few steps behind her when she turned and stopped, quickly, and nearly ran into me. Her free hand gripped my forearm, perhaps to steady herself. She leaned even closer, so close that she was lost in my shadow: "We must be careful what we say in the house."

I resisted the urge to glance at the house, as if it were listening. Even the bugs were waiting. I leaned back slightly to bring some space and light between the two of us. "What do you mean?"

"There is a ghost in the house," she said and took her hand off my arm.

"That's the face, you mean."

She nodded.

"Who is it?"

"A Frenchwoman. I do not know her name. The woman who built the house."

"This was back before the American War."

"Yeah, she's an old ghost. This used to be the house of a French colonial administrator."

"Is she a hungry ghost?" I asked with more concern. Hungry ghosts are ravenous, angry beings who harass the living out of revenge for their wrongful deaths and denied funeral rites. A lot of war dead are hungry ghosts because their bodies were never recovered for proper funerals. Hungry ghosts are skeleton thin, gray-skinned.

They have tiny, puckered mouths and bloated stomachs—cut off from the offerings of their living kin, they can never fully feed themselves and are often unable to move on to another life. They are made vicious by their appetites.

"No . . . she's just French." I didn't know what that meant, but I had a sense of neighborly strangeness. "It's okay if foreigners stay in the guest house, so we thought it would be okay if you stayed here . . . but then I worried that you probably shouldn't be in a house with a ghost by yourself."

All at once, I understood what had felt so odd about the two of us staying at the only guest house in town. "That's why we're the ones staying at the guest house. And everyone else is camping at the clearance site. I thought it was a money issue!"

Vanida shook her head, "They could stay at the guest house, no problem. But they don't want to because of the ghost."

Then I understood the part about Vanida choosing to stay at the haunted house, at what she felt was her own risk, to keep me safe. "Thanks for staying at the guest house with me, Vanida."

She met my half-smile with half of her own. "It's okay, but I think it is better if we are here together. We should have told you about it, instead of letting you stay at the guest house like the other foreigners. I'm sorry. You must be careful what you say around ghosts: if you say bad things, if you say car crash, she might hear you and make it happen out of spite. She could hurt you if she wanted to."

I let that fear slide past me.

"Does Channarong know about the ghost?"

"No, he stays at the senior officers' house."

I nodded, thinking.

I didn't believe in ghosts in the existential sense of an afterlife, but I did believe in their cultural reality and ability to affect people's experiences. In the study of culture, ghosts are real in every way that matters. This was especially true in this old battlefield: ruins layered beneath everyday life, and there was a very real sense in which people were being haunted by histories of imperialism and war. I understand ghosts as ways that violent, unresolved pasts manifest in society like unconscious thoughts in the mind. The names or words that a society has silenced still speak themselves in the mouths of ghosts.

I remembered sitting with Chantha on the porch of her apartment in Vientiane. The city was under curfew: it was common to see armed men on patrol or at checkpoints. She had looked up and down the street, scanning for police and military men. Then she had pointed at the trees above us and said, "Be careful! In Laos, even the trees have tongues." Large, thick-barked trees overhung her porch. Their long, sinuous, green seedpods were called lin mai in Lao, literally *tree tongues.* Police harassment, spies, surveillance, corruption, and extrajudicial violence like disappearances, reeducation centers, and secret prisons were an expected feature of Lao society. Many of these terror techniques had been practiced by the French colonialists, or were later brought into Laos by American paramilitary trainers during the Secret War. Laos' history of imperial warfare and more recent authoritarian violence are twin ghosts: they are both forms of state terror, methods of haunting a population through fear and force. Imagine if the trees were listening to us.

Another thought occurred to me. "Is that why you bought incense yesterday at the market?"

"Yes, I plan on using them for prayer."

She pulled three sticks of incense out of the package, still gripped in her hand. "Will you help me place these by the front door?"

"Sure. Do we need to light them first?"

"Yes, but I am not a monk," she demurred, "I think it is enough for us to just pray."

Vanida thought it best for us to place our incense by the first step of the front porch stairs. And to feed the ghost, she laid out a bowl of sticky rice and a little of the fried crickets. I followed her lead: we nodded out heads in silence for a few minutes. I thought about Laos' history of colonialism without precisely praying. At my feet, the small embers were like tiny fireflies, and the blue smoke of the incense mixed with the cool breath of night through the garden.

I first learned about the appetites of ghosts from Chantha. Back in Vientiane, she had invited me to her neighborhood wat for Boun Haw Khao Padapdin, a festival for feeding the spirits of the dead.

Chantha described the festival to me this way: "After you die, if you did bad things, there is a place like a large house where you go. Each room is a different bad thing: there is a room for adultery, a room for robbery, a room for other things. On this day, all the doors of the house are open. And every spirit can come out and eat."

"Actually, that sounds terrifying!" I told her. I imagined hordes of specters just out of sight, waiting to pounce and devour me.

"Yes, that is because your culture is bad about feeding ghosts so yours are very hungry. So you are afraid of ghosts." Chantha scooped coconut sweets onto ovals of banana leaf, laying the leaf platters among the roots of a sacred tree growing on the temple grounds. For each platter, she unscrewed the cap from a water bottle, presumably so the ghosts wouldn't have to struggle with disembodied hand coordination, poured a first sip for the spirits of the earth, and then laid the uncapped bottles by the coconut sweets. "In Laos, we are compassionate with our ghosts."

Chantha hadn't told me to bring food to feed my own ghosts—I wondered where mine resided, if they were present at all—and I felt a bit like an empty-handed guest at a potluck. As if she sensed this, Chantha handed me the basket of coconut rice and the scoop. She gestured for me to help her lay out the platters.

"By being here today, you are making offerings to the very first spirits of your family. It is good that you are American."

"What do you mean?"

"Because Americans have many ghosts to feed."

Riding my bike home, the route back to my house was lined with offerings of fruit, rice, pastries, and cigarettes. I saw the city anew:

the locations of ghosts were visible, and there were at least as many ghosts as there were living humans. Trees, electricity poles, shops, houses all seemed to have ghosts to be fed. All at once, I realized that it was a city shared among the living and dead.

There's bug music coming through the walls. Love songs, the only thing she listened to. I finished putting away the leftovers in the fridge, leaving the limes to soften on the counter. In the kitchen, the cooling coal stove spilled damp smoke, a smudge across the mismatched, broken cutlery. Searching the diamond patches of light pulled through the woven-mat roof, I looked for her. The bug was vibrating its wings, a sound that sped up when it was warm, dancing and singing at the same time. I turned the corner of the villa and found my way to the rose garden: the roses, all red, were sharply pointed and tight, only swollen buds, like spear slashes in the air, blood behind. It was the beginning of dry season and the garden still had a bit of green in it. The village dogs beyond the fence were barking, meaning something was there that I couldn't see but that they had noticed. Dogs barked at ghosts. Among the old rose vines, I found two molded plastic chairs and a small table set with twin cups of espresso.

The cricket was perched on the table, as if composing for her alone. The male cricket, a perfect specimen for eating, was the length of my palm, brown striated with gold, twin spheres for eyes in a rectangular face, antennae alert, huge legs scissoring. The familiar song hummed a delicate yearning through my body. I had the thought that this was the creature that was chewing into my room, growing larger night after night: What had it been eating? In these cycles of death and rebirth, everyone ate everyone else at least once. So I reached out to touch the cup—real after all, hard and warm—but did not bring the espresso to my mouth. Recognizable smell of instant coffee, premixed with sugar. I sat down, across from the empty chair.

Her shoulders were wide in my imagination, when I tried to dream up a life for a French woman on the frontier of empire. I imagined her worn body, hardened by the obligations of raising a European household without the resources of regular trade or supply. Did she know that she had a choice, that France was not the only sivilai, civilization? Her gown, a pale-yellow house dress with buttons from neck to hem, I imagined she had sewn herself of Lao silk. The dress was torn at the shoulder, exposing a sliver of white flesh. In her hand there was a fan of woven bamboo, wafting foreign perfume. She's proud, sitting straight, booted heels crossed, but distorted, a photograph warped by age.

Talking and listening, talking and listening, and now the bugs were listening. Still, silent, the cricket's wings.

I thought about Vanida's insistence that we pray, but I shook my head, "I don't know what to say."

I tried to envision the Frenchwoman's face, but my imagination wavered. Instead, I saw Chantha's face, intelligent and kind. There were so many things that I had never said to her. The two of us had only shared half a language between us: my conversational Lao and her professional English. All of our conversations were sincere rehearsals, practice for what we wanted to say later, when we had the words. I wanted to tell her that I understood her ambitions, that my family's history had also been poor. My mother, the child of immigrants, grew up in a trailer park, and before that, in a poor Jewish neighborhood in New York City. The family fled war-ravaged Eastern Europe for the American metropolis and exchanged one kind of poverty for another. I never met them, my ancestors that crossed the Atlantic by choice. But I felt the weight of their ambitions—their labor for a future that they would never experience. I was the first person in my mother's family to obtain a degree, or a doctorate, or write a book, and I didn't understand my mother. I wanted to tell Chantha that she wasn't the only one moving toward a future out of reach from her family: that now her mother was her ancestor.

Where were the Frenchwoman's bones? Who else fed her spirit? There was no French graveyard. There were only the pillars of family shrines at the wat, the vases of cremated ashes and carefully prepared bones, offerings of juice and coffee, cigarettes, and flowers left to feed the ghost. Had she married into a local family? Was one of the shrines for her? And then I realized that I was at the shrine. This was it: two cups of espresso in the rose garden.

We were eating in the attached outdoor kitchen under the halo of the single bare bulb.

"So, what do you know about the ghost, Vanida? Who was she when she was alive?"

This was a common way to exorcise ghosts in Laos: uncover their histories, acknowledge the violence that had been done to them, and tie up their loose ends if they had any. If ghosts were real, I thought, then maybe it would mean something for me to know her story.

Vanida tittered, unusually cautious, and put her napkin over her mouth. She whispered to me under her hand: "Careful, the ghost is listening!"

"But we're not in the house." I could sense the large, open sky above us and the night tumbling down the mountain into the valley below.

She loosened a bit, clearly still apprehensive, stirred her stew with her spoon, and then ate a few bites. We had made sticky rice and a green eggplant stew with ginger.

"I hear that she was murdered by her husband, the French administrator."

"So that's why she's stuck in Laos," I said, leaning back in my chair. "She died here, but her family all went back to France?"

"Exactly. French women move with their husbands. She's far away from home." She patted her mouth with her napkin and then refolded it back into a square in her lap. I assume that Vanida had learned to eat like a European at her family's hotel.

"Are ghosts dangerous?"

"It depends. They're like snakes in the grass. You have to be careful because they're always listening, they're always there even if you can't see them."

I joked: "Well, maybe she's listening to us now."

And then the lightbulb went out, spooking us both into silence.

6

If a person is working in a factory that produces cluster bomblets, and if there is a malfunction with the fuse or the cooling explosive as it drips into its case, or if the warm oils soak into the person's skin and their clothing, and if they take a smoke in the slick heat of a parking lot in a Kansas summer, then the spark of their lighter might light them up.

If a person is kneading a white fistful of c-4 explosive clay for a controlled demolition, and if there is a thunderstorm charging the air with invisible sparks, one of those sparks could ignite the explosive. I heard of a Lao technician who ate c-4 as a ritual for power, like moonshine steeped with scorpions, and for a time, I imagine that person was a fuse.

If a person is using nitroglycerine patches for chest pain, and if they have a heart attack, and if the emergency responder places paddles on their chest without first checking for and removing the patches.

If a person carries a bomb on their person, keeping the trigger in their coat pocket or giving it to a friend, and if they go to the American embassy and press that trigger.

If a person is being cremated, and if the attendants do not check for and remove any medical devices like pacemakers.

If a person's home is bombed, and if fragments of the explosives lodge in their body and if they make it to the Baghdad hospital, and if the surgeon on duty does not properly account for the fragments. In army guidelines revised for the Middle East wars, the American military recommends sacrificing these potentially explosive patients for the sake of preserving the surgical facility and team.

If these fragments are not properly removed, even if they are inert, they will continue to slice through the person's body for years after the blast, extending the explosion, caught in their inexorable trajectories.

A swarm of gnats, each moving separately but holding together in a perfect sphere, hovered above Dao's empty chair. Beyond the chair, the precipice of the waterfall began; the green hedge sharply broke and fell away. Up rose a white mist, a stage curtain lazily rippling in the updrafts, so dense in places that it obscured the other side of the ravine.

"Sabaidee."

Dao slumped in the chair heavily, legs loose. Shocked, the gnats dispersed and reformed a few feet away. Her shining hair had slipped from her braid like the release of a waterfall. She slowly removed her gloves, one finger at a time, to reveal startlingly clean hands.

"How's the dem today?"

"It's a hard one: the bombs are under all these rocks and tree roots that we have to remove or cut away first. If the land has grown over them for many years, it's very dangerous."

The rest of her team came carrying a large woven mat and began to set up a picnic of coffee and snacks around us. Hot water was fetched in a kettle from a nearby house. The team's chatter was soothing and light-hearted. Khamkhen came last, tying a checkered scarf crosswise from his left shoulder to waist. Seeing him, a few other technicians pulled scarves or string from their pockets and similarly tied themselves. Surprised by this sidestep into ritual, I had no scarf or string to tie. Lacking scissors, two of the technicians tied themselves with the same piece of string: the slender cord connected them like snap peas, born of the same mother vine.

Another chair was brought, and, bowing respectfully, the technicians made room for Khamkhen to sit among them. Before working as a bomb technician, Khamkhen had been a monk at the peace temple above this waterfall. He was an older man of learning, and his age and training gave him a higher status among the bomb techs. He was entitled to sit above us, and if another technician had walked past, she might have bent to keep her head lower than his. Never one to turn down an opportunity for ritual, Khamkhen had invited the team to participate in the religious life of his old temple while they worked in the village. I understood that the team's assignment was an opportunity for him to reconnect with his spiritual brothers and to pass their blessings onto his clearance teammates.

The rhythm of the group chatter slowed and became more considered. No one seemed to notice or mind that I lacked a scarf. Only Khamkhen and Dao had chairs, while the rest of us reclined on the woven mat. Despite her lower status, Dao kept her chair because her left leg made it difficult for her to sit on the ground.

"This work is often hard," I ventured, not sure if we were still talking about clearance. I realized that I had lost the thread of the conversation. Without responding to me, the others quieted further.

"You do it now, Khamkhen. You are the oldest," a young boy named Simok piped up. The earnest boy had a piece of yellow plastic cord tied shoulder to waist—a remnant from the cords used to mark rows in explosives surveys.

Khamkhen nodded, closed his eyes briefly, took a deep breath, and laid his palms down slowly on his knees. The group settled, expectant. I slowly realized that this was the beginning of a basi sukhuan, called basi for short, a ritual for calling back and concentrating one's khuan, or *body spirits*. The basi is a ubiquitous ritual for positive welfare, especially in moments of transition or crisis when one's khuan might flee the body. It is a ritual of physical and social fullness, when a person asks their friends, family, and colleagues to help bring any wayward spirits back into their body. The assembled kin together solidify the physical and social body of the person at the core of the ritual. I loved that the basi treated personhood as porous among one's social group, partially dependent on the care of others. But this model of the person was so different from the rugged individualism of the American West that it also raised concerns for me about the possibility of wholeness—was complete fullness possible if one's self was fragmented across many selves and could be amputated or lost? I had missed a crucial notice about today's ritual, perhaps an unrecognized gesture or silent glance, and I did not know who would be at the center of this basi.

Khamkhen began singing scriptures in Pali, softly at first and then louder. His assured voice recited the words in carefully practiced tones that resonated, expanding out from our small group, out past the edge of the cliff to accompany the deep rumble of the waterfall. As he sang, he drew cut lengths of white cotton string from his pocket and showed them to us. A gift from his temple brothers.

Many people could recite scriptures from memory, but few monks, and fewer laypeople, understood Pali. It's the Church Latin of Theravada Buddhism. Monks learned to recite scripture for the sound, not the translation. The recitation itself was considered soothing and curative—akin to tuning an instrument. Vibrations in the air, and in our bodies, create an awareness of a shared field of force. I thought of the feeling at a high-powered rock concert in California: similarly, I would feel the vibrations move through the floor, up through my feet, and from my hands to the hands of my partner. The boundaries between people dissolved into ripples of sound.

Simok reached out to lay his palm on Vanida's shoulder, and Vanida reached out to lay her palm on my shoulder, and the rest of them reached their arms out, all our arms shaping a mandala with Dao at the center. Without having it explained, I knew that this basi was for Dao. I was sitting closest to her, and when my palm touched her shoulder, as if waiting for the sign, Dao offered her hand to Khamkhen with her delicate wrist up, the blue line of her pulse exposed.

He placed the string at her wrist, briefly pressing her pulse with his thumb, and intoned in Lao: "May you be strong as the antlers of a stag..."

...he brushed the string down her palm to the tips of her fingers...

"...as strong as the tusks of an elephant..."

...and he brushed the string again from her wrist to the tips of her fingers...

"...may every obstacle be removed from your path..."

...the gentle brushing continued, it was like sweeping dust out of a room...

"...may all illness leave you and be replaced with complete health and happiness!"

And finally he tied the basi string at her pulse, knotted three times.

The company intoned the blessing "Satu, satu!" and let their arms fall back, the mandala opening like the many thin petals of a chrysanthemum. Turning toward their neighbors, people began to tie basi strings around each other's wrists.

"May I?"

"Yes, please," Dao said and offered me her other wrist.

"May you be strong as the antlers of a stag..."

I struggled to remember the exact phrases that Khamkhen had used mere moments before. Under my hands, Dao's fingers flexed, now the athletic fingers of a technician who handled explosives.

"May you be as strong as the tusks of an elephant... may all illness leave you and be replaced with complete health."

I felt her pulse beneath my thumb as I tied the triple knot over her wrist. "Satu."

"Thank you. May I return the blessing?"

"Yes, Dao, I would like that."

I was surprised by the delicacy of the string ends on my palm, like the whiskers of a horse. The feeling drew me into my skin and my animal body.

Dao's blessing for me was different: "May you be as intelligent as an elephant and with an elephant's memory for home . . . may all obstacles leave your path and your travels always be easy. Satu!"

"Thank you." I felt within myself for a renewed sense of fullness. Through my knees and feet, I could feel the crumbling earth beneath the rush mat. I could feel a glistening wetness from the waterfall thinly moistening my clothes and skin.

Around us, the others were murmuring their own blessings for each other. The waterfall endlessly pounded mist into the air. Coffee was brewed and cups passed from person to person. I passed Dao a cup of thick, unfiltered coffee.

"Lao baw mi jaleun," Dao murmured over her coffee. At first, I wasn't sure that she was speaking to me. *Laos cannot progress.* Or, translated differently, she might have also meant *Laos cannot become developed,* or even might have meant, *Laos does not have spiritual power.* I had heard the word jaleun used by aid workers to describe development projects like roads and markets. But I'd also heard this word used by monks at temples to describe spiritual power. Jaleun described a being's ability to attain its fullest positive expression, usually understood in terms of Buddhist enlightenment, but also often understood in terms of wealth, physical well-being, or political influence. If a being lacked jaleun, it would never be fully whole or satisfied. These multiple meanings rolled around in my thoughts like marbles.

Explosives clearance was very precise—specialized equipment, software, and expert staff—and was also always incomplete. "I can certify danger, but not safety," Channarong once told me. In Laos, the difference between danger and safety could be extremely thin: clearance teams sometimes only cleared down to twenty-five centimeters, the depth of a typical Lao plow. There were always more bombs beneath.

Dao sighed and shook her head, repeating, "Lao baw mi jaleun."
I looked at her quizzically. "What do you mean?"

"We don't have the necessary capacity." She cocked her head to the side, smiling hesitantly at me. She was wearing the same blue canvas jumpsuit as every other technician, but she had secured her braid using two hair clips decorated with purple bows. "Laos is like a bucket with a crack in the bottom: we try and try to fill it, but the water always empties out. Our projects fail when they might have worked in Thailand. Development doesn't work here because we lack jaleun."

I began to piece together thoughts in my head with earlier words I had heard from Dao about her home village.

"Before you were a technician, you came from a village that was bombed, didn't you?"

"All the villages in the mountains were bombed. But I didn't know that when I was growing up. In my village, people would bring metal back from the woods and use it to make cookpots. We had no markets to buy metal, so it was better to find the metal in the woods and make it yourself."

She cupped her hands together to form a hemisphere. There were many basi strings at each of her wrists, including the one that I had tied for her. "My parents would use candles made out of the defused caps of the BLU-3 cluster submunitions filled with oil and a wick."

Her cupped hands—the shape of an empty bomb.

"I never knew that they were bombs. Never knew what a bomb looked like. I didn't know any better; my parents never talked about the war, and what was there to say about a secret war anyway? All they knew of it dropped out of the sky or flew away. So we knew nothing and could not even tell the history of our own suffering. These might as well be candles, not bombs."

Looj, another young woman, added: "It was the same in my village."

Dao was silent, and we waited together for her to finish her story. Little pandan cakes, bright green, were handed out in their sparkling foil packages. Simok slipped away with coffee and sweets and laid them at the edge of the cliff as an offering to the spirit of the waterfall. There were a few rows of coffee plants growing just behind us, parallel to the falls. Too few to be for commercial use, and I thought that perhaps our coffee came from these plants. A scattering of children gathered there, peeking at us through the bushes. When I looked their way, they laughed and hid their faces.

"Then I found a bomb when I was repairing the house. I hammered a piece of wood into the ground, and there was a bomb underneath, and it exploded."

"My first legs were the ones I was born with. I don't remember my left leg very well. I remember that my legs were different—that one was shorter than the other—but I can no longer remember how. Was this leg shorter or longer? Did I have a scar on my knee from when I fell in the creek? Did my hip hurt when I walked, did my weak ankles slide in the mud? Did I have good balance? Was my pinky toe turned under, did it heal crooked?

"I stretch my legs out in front of me and look at them. My body is covered with tiny scars shaped like grains of rice—these are shrapnel marks where the pieces of the bomb moved through me. Underneath the scars, sometimes I can feel the small pieces left inside. Like feeling small rocks in cooked rice. Like crushing small rocks between my teeth. Sometimes I look at other people's legs and try to match them up: yes, that was like mine, mine was like hers, mine was slender, mine had a knee like that, mine had beautiful toes. But I don't remember anymore. These new prosthetics even me out because now both my legs are the same length."

"My second leg was a bamboo leg made in the style of my home ban. It was narrow, just a piece of wood that ended with a metal cap. When I first made it, the wood was almost the color of my skin. It was very uncomfortable. I didn't want to wear it, but I didn't have a choice if I wanted to move around and keep doing things. There were already two survivors in my ban, and they taught me how to make my left leg by harvesting wood from the forest and pounding aluminum for the cap. There was no way to put on both my shoes, so I would wear through my right shoes only. One of the other survivors told me about a shoe seller at the market who would exchange my lefts for other people's rights, and I went there and I imagined another mountain girl buying my lefts. Sometimes we say that twins are bad luck, but this girl was my lucky twin. I never met her, but she was the other half of my pair of shoes and my pair of legs.

"I would listen to these two older survivors talk. They would debate whether khuan would inhabit our artificial limbs. The monks were not part of this debate, just us.

"And you, anthropologist, do you see these basi strings I tied around your wrist? They are to call back and strengthen your khuan. Khuan are the spirits that keep your body and mind alive. Everyone is born with thirty-two khuan. They can leave your body for a while, but if they go too far, you will weaken and get sick or depressed. No, khuan must not be confused with souls or possessing ghosts: khuan don't reincarnate and aren't personal. They are the force that makes a living body different from a corpse. It's like the beat in your heart—that is one of your khuan.

"When the bomb exploded, it scared these spirits out of my body, and I was very sick for a while after the explosion. I still worry that I don't know how many khuan I lost: Do I have only thirty, or twenty-five? It is the sort of thing a spirit doctor would know.

"One of the survivors in my ban, I remember he said: 'I think they just go away and are lost forever, and that is why our lives are so hard.'

"But the other survivor said, 'I think they might come back but must be invited by a doctor. It is like any spirit ceremony, but the doctor must be very convincing to entice the khuan back. The new leg must be very nice—clean and well made.'

"I thought that the second man's leg was much nicer. He had painted his leg with his wife's indigo for weaving. The cap was padded with leather scraps.

"These two old men sat by the village office from dawn to dusk, offering their opinions on everything. They did not have jobs, but they did have opinions. They carried twin stools with them, made of the same tree as their legs, and sat their stools at a well-worn spot in the shade. Sometimes, I saw them take off their legs and massage their stumps with tiger balm. My leg didn't look like theirs: my skin was still red and soft, but their legs were old and well worn, with callouses like on the heels of their feet. My mother tried to get me to make a stool of my own and join them—I ignored her.

"My mother tried to get me out of the house as much as possible because she was worried I would bring bad luck onto whatever she was doing. I wasn't allowed to help with any cooking, and my brothers refused to eat the food if I touched it first. They were worried that I would bring the misfortune of another explosion.

"They'd say, 'Oh, she's put bad luck in the soup!' It made me sad and I would often cry.

"I felt angry because they ate their soup with spoons made of war scrap found in the jungle—we called them war spoons. The wooden mold for the spoons was carved to look like the cheap silverware at the Chinese market in the valley, but where those spoons said CHINA, these spoons said LAOS. My brothers would push these war spoons into their mouths!"

"My third leg was given to me for free, a gift from the army.

"Before the war, the French would send doctors on donkeys up to our ban. They would make us take vaccinations and other medicines. After the revolution, the Lao army came up these same paths, but their donkey had a cart full of fake legs. There seemed to be an extra leg for everyone in this new Laos.

"The army men saw the three of us on our stools in the shade: the two old survivors and me, with our opinions and no jobs.

"A young soldier, who still had all his arms and legs, came up to us and said, 'The victorious state thanks you for your sacrifices, honorable soldiers,' bowed, handed us three legs, and left with his donkey. It happened so fast, I didn't have time to tell him that I wasn't a soldier!

"These legs were lightweight, made all of aluminum, and all the same size and length. They were thin, more like pegs than legs, with a leather harness at the cup. Mine was too long and I could barely use it. I wondered if it was made like the war spoons were made, from war scraps found in the jungle. I think they were made from explosives, the same that unmade the legs. So I thought it was a bad luck leg, and I gave it to my brothers who melted it down to make their cookpots. My brothers, they consumed the war, they put it in their mouths; I let them melt this leg into a pool of sticky silver since they believed they could control their luck."

"My fourth leg was barely mine before the doctor took it away again. She told me that I couldn't have it because it might explode. I told her my leg already exploded, and wasn't that what all legs do, anyway, in this country of a million bombs?

"Another soldier had come up the donkey path and told our chief that any survivors in the ban were entitled to free prosthetics at a new clinic in the city. We told him that we couldn't afford to go to the city, but he said that there was a foreign humanitarian organization that would pay for us to travel to the clinic, too.

"So we three survivors traveled down the mountain together. We took a donkey to help us since it is very tiring walking that far, bobbing up and down on one shoe each. When we reached the road, we hired a tuk-tuk and made sure that the driver wrote us a receipt so we could be reimbursed by the humanitarians. I had never gotten a receipt before for anything.

"The clinic was a small concrete building. I remember that there were many people on crutches hobbling across the tiled patio, from one side to the other, practicing. I noticed their legs: none were made of wood, but all of plastic or polyurethane with actual feet in shoes. There were trees all around, and a pet monkey in one of the trees, and nice tables in the shade where some people were playing checkers. There was a vendor pushing a cart of sugared fruit: jackfruit and melon slices with chili sugar. And I thought, yes, this is a good place, I want to be where people offer me sugared fruit.

"The doctors told us that the British had donated all of their old prosthetics to Laos and Cambodia, and we could have our pick of their legs. I picked one, smooth and lightweight, with a padded cup that fit comfortably around my thigh and a shaft that was the correct length. It was the color of black silk.

"It bothered me a bit that it had been someone else's leg. These British soldiers must be very unlucky, to lose their first legs and then lose their legs again, giving parts of their bodies away that could be used for black magic. I decided it was my responsibility to treat this leg very well, for the interest of myself and this other unlucky person. In my village, we made sure to destroy our nail clippings, hair, and bandages so that bits of ourselves didn't fall into the control of sorcerers. You must be careful not to give parts of yourself away.

"Then, a group of new humanitarians came to the clinic. They made the doctors take the British legs back. They told us that these legs were too advanced for us to use in our villages. They told us that Red Cross international standards recommended that the Lao and Cambodian people only have cheap legs! I asked them many questions, and they told me that they were worried about maintenance since Laos does not have good hospitals. There was a material in the legs that made them lightweight, but that would explode if exposed to the air. The legs had to be kept in very good condition and could only be disposed of in controlled conditions, similar to how we dem explosives. The doctor didn't trust me to keep the black silk leg in good condition—but here I am now, an expert trusted with actual explosives! Yes, I blame the Red Cross for taking this leg from me.

"One of the foreign doctors told me that in places that were unsafe for humanitarians, they would drop the donated prosthetics from aircraft onto the target populations on the ground.

"I thought this sounded horrifying, being hit by falling bombs and then by falling legs. How many legs did they drop—the same number of legs as bombs? Of what kinds—tall people, short people, white people, yellow people? Thinking about this made me angry, and I snapped at the foreign doctor: Why not just drop legs that explode? But she didn't understand what I meant and told me that my black silk leg was too dangerous for Laos. This made me feel even more angry, but I said nothing. I was upset that the black silk leg would go to someone in a country with better jaleun. A country that makes bombs, not a country that is bombed.

"Waiting in that clinic, with all those other people waiting for their own legs, I began not to worry if our khuan found our new bodies. At the clinic, I imagined that I was getting a totally new kind of body that was modern, technically superior, and with new capabilities that I was only beginning to understand. The spirits would have to keep up with my new body."

"My fifth leg was made for the ban. It was a Red Cross leg made from cheap polyurethane with a metal spring joint at the knee. A village leg for village work. It made me sigh, because I felt that this was a leg for moving backwards not forwards. A bad luck leg, but I didn't know how to melt it down into something else.

"It didn't really bend at the heel, so I had to walk slowly and precisely. It was like balancing all the time, and I had to be careful about getting it caught in things since it would slip off. In the rice fields, where we do our women's farm work, it would stick in the mud and slide off. I felt that I was always stepping closer to the day when the ankle would crack. If I couldn't have the black silk leg, I wanted a leg like an elephant's: large and flat, sturdy, that wouldn't slide off in the mud. Elephants are the only other beings with thirty-two khuan; our bodies are alike in this way.

"This Red Cross leg came in a slightly off-yellow color, not a skin color at all, but the boring color of moldy canvas and military uniforms. It was a color that looked stirred-up, like muddy water, and lacked the liveliness of real skin. It looked as if there was nothing inside it, no blood. I could not imagine a khuan recognizing this leg as part of a person."

"My sixth leg is the one I am wearing now. It is my work leg for explosives clearance, and I always wear it while working with my team.

"While I was at the clinic waiting for my village leg, I heard that the local clearance organization had a hiring program for survivors of explosions. The doctor warned me that the job would be dangerous—I almost laughed in her face. I thought that it might be less dangerous than my current job, which was farming rice fields full of bombs. And I was right: I feel safer as a demolition tech than I ever did as a farmer.

"I asked the doctor to help me to apply.

"There was another village man from the mountains, Atith, who also applied even though everyone knew he wasn't a survivor. He lost his arm in a truck accident. The humanitarians still paid for his trip to the clinic and were paying for his arm, too.

"Atith and I both got the jobs. He's an accountant. I'm a technician. My job came with this new kind of leg that had been designed in Cambodia for deminers. It is beautiful, white, and light like bone. All plastic, without any metal parts, so I could walk through the minefields without triggering our metal detectors. It doesn't feel like a leg, but more like a tool; putting it on is like picking up a metal detector or a shovel. It is so smooth that I feel like I am slipping on a special white glove. When I have this leg on, I feel connected to people in Cambodia—it makes me feel good that this leg is designed specifically for me and people like me so that we can clear our villages. I want people to be safe, especially since I wasn't.

"The ground at clearance sites is often uneven because we are digging things up, and I still lose my balance with this leg. For this reason, I am in charge of the safety procedures and trigger mechanisms. So I don't have to balance around the holes.

"They put our picture on a brochure for their donors, Atith and I, do you remember? As if we were both survivors. But it didn't bother me; I had gotten that aluminum leg from the military even though I had never been a soldier. I feel he is just as deserving of this job, and is Atith harming anyone? Only good can come of this misrepresentation. Because we are missing parts of ourselves, people look at us and see the person they want to see.

"The organization hosted a New Year's party at a local tourist hotel. Atith wore makeup and a red hibiscus in his hair. He rolled his hips, lascivious, when he danced. I envied him because I couldn't dance.

"Every evening, before I go to bed, I take off and clean my legs with a damp cloth and store them gently wrapped in cotton in the drawer of a cabinet. I bet I keep better care of my legs than you keep of yours! But none of these other six legs feels natural to me, and I am often sad: I have only one leg, and the other is lost."

My palms still tingled from the basi. I felt the strings tied at my wrists. Dao's arms were wrapped in a handspan of white blessings, one or two from each of her teammates. What is our capacity for wholeness, jaleun? What does it mean to share ourselves among many—our health, our bodies, our possessions? I thought of Dao's lucky twin wearing the other half of her pair of shoes. I thought of Dao's brothers melting war scraps into one large, glistening metal body.

I once brought a bag of giveaways to the office—a few cooking implements that I couldn't use in my studio kitchen and some castoff clothes. A pair of foam slip-ons. Dao had taken the kitchen spoons but refused to consider the clothes and shoes. "You must be careful about what you give away," she said with concern and drew me to the trash can instead. "The things we own always have bits of ourselves in them, and it is dangerous to give bits of yourself away. It is safer to throw stuff away—tear it up, and make sure you put it in the trash yourself." Like a mother, she watched me while I ripped up and dirtied my old clothes.

I felt pass over me curtains of mist from the waterfall, flowing from the gate of the temple.

Khamkhen's peace temple was celebrated for its concrete Buddha statues made from sand molds, each mold unique and only used once for each Buddha. The sand was harvested from the base of the waterfall and carried by hand up the foot track to the temple. Sometimes the molds failed, and the statues came out with broken limbs: these maimed statues were stored in a special place on the temple grounds, a kind of spiritual hospital for the unmade. A temple is a safe place to store bad luck. The complete statues were sanded and painted gold, but the broken ones were left unsurfaced, gray concrete. The monks pray for the broken. Before I knew this, I came upon the place and was struck by the mass of shattered bodies, like a scene of gray carnage: Buddhas without legs but with gentle smiles, Buddhas without heads but with hands outstretched in blessing.

7

I HEARD AN AMERICAN BOMB explode in Laos. But months before that fuse ignited, I listened to the sound in a dream.

I do not remember my dream, only my certainty: a bomb exploded because I heard it. In dreams, sounds from waking life shift to a range beyond the audible that we do not hear with our ears. The register of dream sounds is not in decibels, but in our desire to hear what is unspeakable, silenced, or dangerous. Dream sounds are among the vibrating peripheries of human audition, where sounds are felt rather than heard: the ground shakes, the windowpane shatters, the air shimmers with debris, I am ripped apart.

The dream explosion woke me in one massive breath. My ribcage expanded fully, and then I held still, refusing to release the lungful—I was full with waiting. What sounds do we hold in our bodies, and where do we keep them when we sleep? Where do we keep what harms or heals—coal stove crackle, chanted prayer, slapping laundry on river stones, the wind in the fields, cow bell, motorcycle whine, pencil scratches? My coverlet was hot, and I kicked the cotton sheets off my bare legs. The ceiling fan whirred its mindless circles—nothing, no clatter of falling debris, no rattling windows, no sirens or shouts of alarm. I slowly breathed out, listening to my own relieved exhale. I remembered that many-months-ago visit with Channarong, my yearning to understand his fear. Now, finally, I was afraid.

Rising from the bed and walking to my balcony, I looked over the dark houses and, beside them, to the much darker river. A cooling, wet breeze blew and I shivered. The town beyond my window was silent. My dream didn't wake up with me: I could feel it going on under my skin. The heat of the explosion was in my chest, pumping, my heart gushing its blood. I touched the back of my neck and felt grit, brushed bits of debris off my face, felt a rift between my waking and sleeping mind.

There were no streetlights: the town was one seamless mass limned by the softly glowing moon. Here and there, the moon caught its reflection in the muddy streets. Houses slumped, sleeping, into each other; the door of night opened into every room. The dream, my false memory, flitted from roof to roof, hungry and searching. No plume of smoke marred the horizon. No flashing sirens strobed the flat faces of the houses to distinguish one building from any other.

I looked hungrily over the darkling town. I imagined daybreak: the women of the neighborhood would rise to prepare food for the monks' morning almsgiving. The ritual began when the seamstress across the street switched on the single bare bulb in her kitchen and steamed enough sticky rice to share with the block. Then, her neighbor would light a charcoal stove and begin to grill garlic and peppers for a spicy curry. All of this happened before the men of the neighborhood awoke. When the women finished preparing the food, they would lay out mats along the edges of the street, to protect their knees from the mud, and arrange their food in offering bowls. They would not wear any shoes. I imagined a line of monks turning the corner from the temple, processing slowly, each step a meditation.

Monks spent the monsoon inside their temples and rarely traveled more than a day's walk during this season. The flooded fields and muddy paths teemed with seedlings, larvae, fish, and eggs; I've heard that monks stay inside their temples so that they do not inadvertently step on these tiny, precious beings. Because they do not travel during this season, they rely on the women who live around their temples to supply them with food.

Muted by the morning dim, in my mind's eye I saw the monks' saffron robes tinted a deeper, musty brown. The first monk in the procession would stop above the kneeling seamstress. Bowing low, she would spoon sticky rice and curry into his wooden bowl.

In comparison, my mornings were solitary and without blessings. I took my shower via water brought up by a pump that worked when the electricity was running; otherwise, I carried buckets up from the street. There was no mirror, so I combed my hair by feel. I had a small kitchen in my rented room, with tap water that I boiled before use. I traveled with a spoon and a bowl: I would eat my granola, sweetened with soymilk; then, I would boil water, clean the bowl, and drink my tea—a wok-fried green tea from the Northern plantations—from the same vessel. Cleaning my breakfast bowl: a ritual that reminded me I was far from home.

I felt my feet on the balcony and my heart, still shaking. Beyond the town, looking to the river untouched by sleep, I found action that matched the feeling in my chest. Only when I looked at the river did I hear its roar that was ever-present but difficult to distinguish like the background drone of traffic, unheard until an accident hooks the ears. The village sat at the lowland sweep of the river where, during the monsoon, it sped and swelled to eight kilometers across. The monsoon Mekong had a capacity for violence that was compelling, like the dangerous allure of a tornado or an earthquake. People, buffalo, whole villages regularly disappeared under its brown skin.

In Lao, the river is female, and the river is Mae, *mother.* Beginning at its bank downslope from my hotel, the Mekong was so impenetrable that I had no impression of depth, only of incredible length and width. Was it bigger today than yesterday? It was not possible to look up or downstream: the view was too large. Thailand was a thin line pushed to the horizon that rippled dark green as the sun rose. The current started to sparkle where sunrays slipped over the far hills. Out in the faster middle current, an entire tree slipped past, askew, its uppermost leaves still green and fluttering like garlands on a holiday boat at speed. At this distance, it appeared to be a small skiff, though I am sure, up close, it was a forest giant.

The day began to sigh itself awake. Across the street, dawn kindled the blue of roof tiles, the color opening gently as morning glories. There appeared spots of brightness: the seamstress switched on her single bright bulb, her neighbor lit a cigarette and then threw the match into the hungry coals of her stove. Then the sounds of human voices, the fizzle of a female radio broadcaster leading listeners through their morning exercises.

The river moved me in its current, or rather, its speed was so fast that I could not feel it, nor tell where it was carrying me. A fabulous, breathing presence. Rushing here and there, but without ever feeling absent or out of place. It was as if I was already submerged. The river had become the air, or I had become a small fish, breathing under the muddy water.

The roads were patched with pieces of sky, shimmering from every pothole and wheel rut. Dirt roads alternated with shorter stretches of two-lane pavement, raised on earth embankments with culverts to either side. The culverts kept the roads clear during the wet season when the surrounding villages and fields flooded. This seasonal flooding was called the "flood pulse," the pulse of the river through the lowland plains. I pressed my thumb to the pulse in my wrist, imagining the beat of the river through the valley. *Thump-thump*.

The roads were not for the villagers, but for drivers of cargo trucks, developers, and humanitarian workers like Channarong and me in this white jeep. The Japanese built the best paved roads. Laos had been briefly occupied by Japan during World War II. That Japanese imperial project ended when the American atom bomb destroyed Nagasaki. This old occupation had created a tie between the two countries, and Japan was a regular funder of infrastructure projects in Laos. These roads were trade routes across mainland Southeast Asia; Laos was the land in the middle, tight in the vise of the more prosperous countries and their ports. Countryside flying past the window.

Channarong slowed the jeep when we came to the new Japanese bridge. A metal box girder balanced on three rectangular concrete foundations, one on either bank and a single pier between. The Japanese built the deck of wooden beams spaced like railroad ties, plummeting air beneath. There was no guard rail. The metal was corroded a dull red and bleeding bright orange at the bolts. At both ends, I read twin signs in English and Lao: "Funded by the Japan International Cooperation Agency" beneath a stylized image of two white hands clasping. The bridge crossed a tributary of the Mekong, not as large as the river itself but still fast and dangerous. Channarong gently steered the vehicle over the wooden deck. The car wheels made a double *thump-thump*, like a beating heart.

Running parallel were the remains of a second bridge built much earlier under French colonial rule in the mid-twentieth century. Never repaired, all that remained were two derelict stumps on either bank: rotten molars in a gaping mouth. The collapsed metal supports were left where they fell, netting windfallen branches and other refuse, churning the current to a lacey white froth. Bridges rarely survived more than a few monsoons without regular maintenance. This year, the rains were early, and the river was flooding.

I was accompanying Channarong on his field rounds of all the active clearance projects in the valley: four, each at least an hour's drive apart. We had no translators, no consultants, no donors, and no technicians. Just the two of us in the jeep and I got to sit in the front seat for once. His rounds took several days, depending on the state of work at each site. This was paperwork he had to complete with his feet. For me, it was fieldwork: an excellent introduction to the explosives clearance in the river valley.

He was usually a solitary driver. No radio; the only program out here was the local government station, which played a morning exercise program and then patriotic songs on loop. There were a hundred small noises filling the car without filling the silence: the splash of mud from the wheels, windowpanes shaking in the doors, vinyl seats squeaking against the metal frame. And when Channarong shifted gears, I heard a swiftly truncated thud as of a block of marble turning over.

"I like this kind of silence," he said. No other cars were on the road.

Beyond the bridge, we moved through an eerily quiet country lifted from the smooth surface of a mirror—the landscape sliced by the flood, every tree paired with its reflection. The first village past the bridge was partially submerged. On high ground, a few stilt houses stood dry above the pale brown, but most of the village was underwater. Some of the flooded homes had boats tied to their struts, like a pier. The sky radiated a little sunlight that briefly burnished the surface of the mirror-water: the houses floating in thick, churning clouds.

Approaching the village, I saw that the water rose up and over the culvert to coat the road in mud. Channarong kept driving, intending only to skim the flood. He gently steered the jeep forward; ripples from our wheels swept over the mirror-water, turning the clouds to angry thunderheads. As the car eased into the flood, the engine slowed to a purr, and the car's many small sounds softened. There was a new sound: rhythmic lapping from under the vehicle where miniature waves slapped the undercarriage. He could not see the road directly, but it was perceptible by its traces: the space between the trees, a few meters of fence. The road was familiar to him. The hushed landscape was charged with the electricity of an imminent storm. Air heavy, burdened with water and power. I thought about invisible clouds of atmospheric energy accumulating around me, the dangerous sparks that could set off an explosive.

As we drove through the flooded village, I was amazed to see farmers setting up for a market day on a large, rectangular platform raised a few lucky inches above the water—a floating market. The platform's black shadow delicately undulated on the water's surface, flexing like a living thing. Pale bamboo hats textured the crowd, packed brim to brim between the railings. In the thick, a few hands flew up like birds caught by the wing. The platform was hemmed on all sides with a ruffle of slim boats with needle-sharp prows pointing into the wind. My eye found one of the boats: it was a long, hollow sheath of metal with two added wooden seats, half of a discarded long-range fuel tank from a B-52 bomber, dropped, found, emptied, and repurposed. In the bomb boat, two women tucked their red skirts up to their belts, and, settling into their floating shop, began selling cabbages.

I watched a woman with a wide-brimmed bamboo hat maneuver her boat to dock at the platform, signaling to a man selling a half-dozen trussed black piglets. They knew each other: he waved his cigarette-hand amicably, then transferred the smoke to the corner of his mouth. Her mooring line landed with a visible thud at his feet. Each piglet was encased in a bamboo tube, seemingly woven around the animal while it slept, legs neatly pinched underneath. The tubes must tighten as the piglets struggled in these large Chinese finger traps. The bamboo tubes were woven in an intricate hexagonal pattern, startlingly beautiful, that incorporated a little carrying loop at the center back. They were packets of midnight, portable. Each piglet raised its black snout to sniff the women as she stepped over them and onto the platform. She left her shoes in her boat as if she was stepping into someone's home.

A fleet of cabbage leaves floated offshore, making their way toward our jeep from the market, tracing the current that flowed between us.

"Perhaps we should rent a boat?" I joked to Channarong, the first sentence in an hour's driving.

"If we're still working next week, yes. We'll have to fish for bombs."

✿

Higher up the slope of the river valley, our jeep passed through rickety villages carved out of the jungle or squeezed between timber plantations. In upland Laos, the forest is more important than the road—the road is a way for lumber trucks to get from one forest to another. The sky darkened, throwing down a humid light that deepened the green. Large firecracker trees regularly burst along the road, their long flowers remarkable spikes of red against the polished malachite of the foliage. Spitting rain drummed the windshield, drops that broke into patched circles of silver. The road itself was thin and ragged with holes, slopping over many narrow wooden bridges just wide enough for the jeep, bridges that almost certainly would be washed out later in the monsoon.

I sighted a small hand-lettered sign marked "UXO" tagged to a tree by the road above an arrow pointing deeper into the jungle. UXO stands for *unexploded ordnance*, a common euphemism for bombs leftover from old wars. I call it a euphemism because the phrase hides the violence of these weapons as if peace makes bombs less explosive, or as if bombs that explode after a war ends are somehow malfunctioning. Similarly, I noticed that Channarong trained his clearance technicians to talk about bomb explosions as *accidents* rather than the intentional violence of war. I believe that when a bomb explodes, it is never an accident. These euphemisms tie linguistic knots: "There's been an accident: a man died in an unexploded ordnance explosion." I feel that the language of UXO contributes to dangerous international politics that downplay the long-term impacts of war and reduce the responsibilities of the aggressor to clean up their military waste. And yet, UXO has worldwide relevance in treaties, clearance procedures, news reports, and humanitarian projects—all projects that are mostly funded by aggressors, not victims. To counter this minimizing language, I make a point to always refer to these leftover bombs as *explosive* ordnance rather than *unexploded* ordnance, *explosions* rather than *accidents*.

Channarong swerved off and into the underbrush following the arrow, wet branches whacking the car on both sides. We emerged from the bushes into a fallow rice field, carpeted with new weeds. His team had set up a sizeable beige tent at the border of the field beside military-neat rows of smaller tents, a doused campfire, and a trash pit. The team had strung up a laundry line between two trees. When they finished clearing this village, the team would pack their camp up and move to the next site, leaving behind the black circle of their campfire, a tarred trash pit, and fresh craters. In the traces they left behind, their camp was not so different from the village. Stilt houses are also portable; you can dismantle them and reuse the supplies to build yourself a new village.

Channarong drove straight across the field, thumping over the rice paddy walls, and parked the jeep in front of the largest tent, the control point. The team was already off—their jeeps were gone. They were racing the monsoon rain to finish clearance before the farmers planted next season's rice.

Inside the tent, the control point was divided into zones by red tape, each zone labeled in white capitals against a red background: Rest Area, Medic Area, Scrap Metal Pit, etc. Every control point, at every clearance site managed by this operator, was precisely the same. There was a zone for storing explosives in metal briefcases and a zone for stacking metal detectors like rifles. By standard operating procedure, Channarong's team stationed two medics at the control point at all times. The two bored medics lounged, wearing identical jumpsuits, against a cooler storing fresh blood and other supplies. Each wore a matching blue canvas bucket hat, floppy and damp. They nodded at us without changing posture: "Sabaidee dawn sao." *Good morning.*

Channarong ignored them and headed straight to several large maps hung against the far wall showing topographical and satellite views of the clearance site. Historical bombing data was superimposed over the charts, showing possible airstrikes from the Secret War. Another map displayed items that the villagers had found and reported to the clearance team: mostly cluster submunitions, but also a few landmines at the village border. The historical bombing data only loosely matched with found ordnance, giving a sense of puzzle pieces that didn't quite fit. The monsoon rains moved the bombs, making the history less and less helpful with each passing season.

One of the medics pointed to my shoes and offered in Lao: "You'll need galoshes. Don't want to ruin your nice shoes!"

I followed her finger to look at my shoes. I was wearing plastic slip-ons, closed toe, that could be cleaned with a hose. Perfect for mud, I had thought, wrongly.

"Ah, yes, thank you." She handed me a pair of black galoshes, roughly my size. I didn't relish the idea of wearing galoshes without socks, but there it was.

Channarong was looking at a grid map showing the team's progress through the clearance zone. A grid of ten-by-ten meter boxes overlaid the strike. He turned to one of the medics, asking in English: "Where are they now?"

"They're still in the rice field—here." She pointed to a grid box, still white, at the edge of a zone of red and yellow boxes.

His mouth twisted into a familiar, resigned frown. He turned to me. "They're behind schedule. They're not going to have time to meet us here; we must go out to them. The rainy season makes it hard to do clearance properly, and they are under a lot of pressure from the farmers to finish before planting starts. If they don't finish this year, they'll have to start over again from scratch with surveys next year. The rain moves the bombs, you see, so the surveys only last a year for these flood areas. I've been watching the skies all week. We have to move very fast."

The control point was carefully positioned just outside the blast radius of any explosion that might occur at the clearance site: if something exploded and we were at the control point, we'd be safe.

I followed Channarong, who was walking briskly ahead of me, into the blast zone beyond the control point. I felt my dream shake a little inside me, but I was fully awake, and the dream stayed quiet. At first, I saw tall, red lilies blooming between the trees, but then I found their symmetry and recognized them: red stakes marked the corners of each clearance box. They formed lines through the uneven trees, similar to the careful parterres of a formal garden. The grid map had been replicated, at a one-to-one scale, on the ground. Technicians literally walked through the map, box by box, applying a layer of order to the loose soil of everyday life. Looking down the lane of red stakes, I saw a woman in a navy jumpsuit standing with a clipboard. She had on a bucket hat with the rain flap down to protect her neck and shoulders. She was facing away from us, her back to the wind.

As we approached, I noticed that she and I were wearing identical black galoshes.

Channarong called to her: "Sabaidee, Khamvongsa."

"Hello, Channarong," Kham replied, not smiling. "We're behind schedule."

"I know. It's a tough site. Show me what you've been up to."

Kham nodded once, laying the clipboard flat between the three of us at waist height. I took an edge, holding the fictional table steady. The thin rain was starting to slant sideways onto the map, diluting the markers to watercolor. It was hand-drawn with pencil, colored with florescent highlighters in yellow, red, and green. She was using a one-foot American ruler made of cheap orange plastic.

"This stake is this one . . ." She gestured definitively with her ruler to the nearest red stake, to take its measure, then to its corresponding location on the map. "We're about three-quarters done with the predicted strike."

I interjected: "How do you know that you're three-quarters of the way?"

Her cool, agate eyes dissected the map. "The bomb footprint looks like an egg or a basket of eggs. Do you see?"

"Yes." I circled two long ellipses with my finger. Two eggs.

"You can see the strike: they are two little ovals. The airplane was coming from this direction." She swooped her ruler over the map, mimicking the airplane that dropped those bombs forty, maybe fifty years ago. "I think there will be another footprint here. So, going by the curve of the strike that we've found so far, we can predict the total size. By that measure, we're three-quarters done."

To do these calculations, technicians practiced a sinister form of connect-the-dots where each red dot is a live bomb, a bomb fragment, a crater, or a deadly explosion. Taken together, these red dots often form ellipses, large egg-shaped ovals, that vary by munition type, terrain, and speed or altitude of release. The older the strike, the harder it is to predict their shape. While imprecise, these ellipses can be helpful when combined with data gathered during field surveys.

"Kham, all the members of this team are women, right?" I had heard that we would be working with the only all-female clearance crew in Laos and hoped Kham would talk to me about how her crew had formed.

"Yes, it's a specially funded all-female clearance team." She said it fast in English as if it was just one word: spec'ly-funded-all-female.

"What do you think about that?"

There was a small pause, marked by the subtle twitch of one corner of her mouth. "I think it is good that we have funding for another clearance team; it doesn't matter if the searchers are male or female. It's all the same work. We're surveying this box now." She pointed with her ruler at a technician. "You can go watch Vanida search if you'd like. She's having trouble in her box—lots of trash." A request for us to go bother someone else.

Channarong steered us between two red stakes and into an adjacent box, edging closer to the border of Vanida's active box. We're not allowed to be in the box with her, but we could get close enough to distinguish the sound of her metal detector easily. Almost immediately, Vanida's detector started pinging loudly. She knelt to dig, by hand, around the sound.

Channarong added a whispered commentary: "She's digging on signal. We're safe here. Ten meters is the required safety distance."

Ten meters was also the width of each survey box—the width of risk. Closer than ten meters and severe injury or death were near certainties. Kham had cut the whole site into ten-meter boxes. We walked through a map whose key was human mortality.

Channarong had his arms folded in front of him, lounging at an angle. He said dismissively, still whispering: "You can tell that she's a new girl because she is wearing makeup and gold earrings. Once they've been here for a while, they care less about that kind of stuff."

I gave him a hard look, uncomfortable with this casual misogyny, but he didn't see my expression. He continued to provide commentary.

"Small sound. That sound is too small to be a cluster bomb."

Vanida was moving off the sound already. "Ah, she knows."

A few steps and she found another sound, longer. She scraped her boot over the soil to clear the signal and see if it was surface trash like a beer can. She spiraled her detector over the area, pinpointing the sound. Putting her detector down, she took up her small trowel and slowly dug a hole, pushing the soil behind her so that it didn't interfere with her forward direction through the box. She found a small piece of metal and tossed it into an orange bucket.

Channarong noticed something about the item—the sound—and came over to pick it up. When Channarong entered her safety zone, Vanida stopped moving, wary, stiff, and one knee half-bent. Protocol dictated that she cease activity until her box was secured—only one person per box. Every clearance technician was a chess piece in its square: there was a risk that Channarong might disturb ordnance she had exposed or that they would both be injured if an ordnance exploded. She stood still, detector leaning against her thigh. Head cocked under the brim of her rain hat, she followed him under lidded eyes until he had moved past the red perimeter. Only then did her arms relax, letting the detector fall slightly to the side of her thigh. She repositioned the detector and resumed her search.

Channarong showed the item to me: it was a large aircraft artillery cartridge. About the size of my index finger, rusty orange. It was nearly three times as large as the little rocket I had picked up from dad's window sill as a child.

"What does this item tell you about this site?" I asked.

"Well, there was probably ground fighting. It could have been shot from an airplane at ground troops. But we already know from historical records that this site was bombed. Maybe it was dropped before the battle, or the battle was abandoned, and they dropped their cargo? Maybe this was a storage site? It is old, almost certainly from the war."

He handed the cartridge to me. I fiddled it between my fingers, jostling its weight. Then handed it back to Channarong, who again entered Vanida's safety zone. Vanida froze in an awkward pose with her knees half-bent. She and I both knew that people weren't supposed to be in the same active clearance box at the same time. Channarong didn't seem to notice her discomfort. He crossed, tossed the cartridge back into Vanida's orange bucket, then crossed back.

Another signal. She dug down, found nothing, and moved on—a few steps later, another suspicious signal. This pattern continued for the next several meters. She was quickly tilling the earth in her wake, like a farmer in her fields before planting. Digging through layers of history: the war was one layer, buried between layers of flooding, rice farming, and village construction. And farther down, traces of older ways of life, people that died decades or centuries before Vanida was born. Searchers sometimes dug up archaeological artifacts from that part of human history before airstrikes, tanks, artillery guns, or agent orange. Pummeled into the earth, the bombs pierce these older layers, making a ruin of history.

"Vanida was number one in her EOD class," Channarong whispered. EOD, Explosives Ordnance Disposal, are training programs for safely handling and demolishing ordnance in the field. Trade secrets of the clearance technicians. International organizations developed courses for specific battlefields. In Laos, EOD classes focused on Secret War–era ordnance, mostly cluster munitions and other remains of air warfare. If Vanida wanted to go work in the modern battlefields of Syria, for example, she'd have to take an EOD class for Syrian ordnance. Class ranks were a point of pride, like being college valedictorian.

"Yeah, and what were you?"

"I was number five."

To our right, there was a commotion in an adjacent box. A searcher found a fragment of a cluster submunition, soon confirmed by Kham. Immediately, the searcher in the box stopped, collected her equipment, and moved on to the next box. Kham recorded the item's GPS coordinates on her map and marked the submunition with a tall blue stake. The entire survey process for that box took about seven minutes.

A distant crack of thunder vibrated half the sky, northwest. All together, the team looked to the sound, above the red stakes, the rice fields, and the thin trees—to the clouds advancing from the far mountains down to the river valley. If the storm got too close, they'd have to stop clearance. The risk of atmospheric sparks triggering explosions made demolition near thunderstorms too risky. The northwestern sky was the color of boiled snow; billowing gray clouds tinged white at their peaks. When it made landfall, the storm's monumental feet would plow the earth into rivers.

Now Vanida was very far behind her counterparts in the other boxes. Channarong whispered: "I've made her nervous. Let's go intimidate some of the other new searchers."

"Channarong, what do you think about having all-female teams?"

"I think it's silly. Gender equality is not as simple as just making it possible for women to be clearance technicians. The team is losing its funding this season, and then most of these women will be out of a job because they were only hired for the all-female team. That's why Kham is so nice to you—she thinks you're a donor! Most of them won't become technicians on other teams. For most of them, this is their last project. It's not an effective strategy."

"What is an effective strategy, in your opinion?"

"Women need to be equally represented in the leadership of the teams and the organization. We're shifting a whole history of men being in charge; there's a lot of young men training to be leaders or moving through the ranks. But it's only in the last few years that we've started training women. They're not yet moving through the ranks! Kham is our only female team leader in this province. Vanida is our only female translator. That's a lot of history to shift! Early operators were all cowboys, macho men who were high on risk."

Soldiers are like that, too, I thought.

"Yes, I've met those macho men." Another research liaison I'd worked with was an older white man who thought it appropriate to exchange research permissions for sexual privileges. That man called me "dear" in his late-night illicit, unasked for, unanswered texts and phone messages. His hands slipping down my back, my thigh, my arm, or on my shoulder, a small pull toward him. If we worked a site together, he'd make a point to always pee in the bush near me. He'd turn around, eyes on me, hands on his groin, while he zipped up his pants. All the managers at that organization were older white men, ex-military. When I left that project, I changed my phone number and my hotel. Back in the capital city, I joked to my Lao friends: "The men are more dangerous than the bombs!" I chose to never again work with that clearance organization, which meant that I was no longer able to research the provinces they controlled.

Channarong pointed behind us to the tent covering the control point. "Back then, there was no control point, no medics on watch, no safety gear. There were a lot of accidents, and a lot of people died because they thought safety was for cowards and women! Old school operators: a room full of swinging dicks. In the military, I think many of them learned a certain gender dynamic that made them want to be leaders of men. I think clearance attracts a certain kind of man who wants to lead other men. You know that joke about the fireman, the policeman, who walks into a bar? Well, these clearance men wanted to be the biggest badass of them all, to say: I defuse live bombs."

His focus shifted to me: "Do you carry pepper spray in your purse?"

I never told anyone about the harassment from my former research liaison. There was no one to tell since he had been my only superior at that organization. "Yes, I do."

"That's good. That's good to hear."

That was the first, and only, time that a male technician warned me to be careful about harassment. I remembered it: the only time that a man had done the work that I do as a matter of ethics and training, the imaginative work of understanding the risks of another person's life. But I wondered, thinking about the way Channarong casually walked through Vanida's safety zone, how far did his imagination extend?

At our feet, a blue stake marked a small harvest of BLU-26 cluster submunitions, a type of bombie that I called "spiral arm galaxies" for the spiral shape of their fluted edges (bombie is a Lao word for cluster bomblets). The rain made the mud slick over the items, softening their outlines.

A whistle sounded over the field, then Kham's voice via loudspeaker: "Break!"

All at once, searchers stopped. The field seemed to suddenly empty. Birdsong replaced the ping of the detectors. Many searchers sat where they were, in the weeds.

Vanida walked our way, holding her detector with the handle pointed toward me. She smiled broadly, pale lipstick, her smile raising her lightly powdered cheeks to the corners of her eyes.

Her American English was perfect and precise: "Hello! I am glad to meet you. I hope that you had a good morning. Do you want to try the detector?"

"Okay."

There was a long shaft with an armrest, like on a crutch, above an ergonomic handle. I placed my arm on the armrest and wrapped my fingers around the handle, lifting the device out of her hands. It was much heavier than I thought it would be. Fifteen pounds? But the thing was weighted cleverly so that it leaned into position in front of me like an extension of my arm. I was reminded of the invisible dog trick: a leash stiffened with wire, shaped and weighted to drag in front of the clown as if there were a real dog in the harness. I set my detector in front of me, taking my invisible dog for a walk.

Vanida stepped in and adjusted the reach of the arm so that it fit my height. I noticed a slim gold bracelet on her left wrist.

"Thank you."

Now, the head of my detector was about ten centimeters above the ground. Turning to my audience, I asked in Lao, "Do I look like a searcher?"

The surrounding women laughed. "Ngaam lai!" *Very pretty*, one woman said, and the others took up the words: "Ngaam lai, ngaam lai . . . !"

Vanida, number one in her EOD class, gently corrected me: "No, not yet, you should have it about five centimeters above the ground. And then sweep it back and forth . . ."

She put her cell phone on the ground. I obligingly swept my detector over the phone—a loud piiiiing!

"Now that you have found it, you can pinpoint the sound by sweeping in a circle over the area to see how big the thing is."

I circled my detector, "hearing" the edges of the phone as changes in pitch. The sound increased in pitch and duration when I was right on top of the phone, and then slowly dwindled to nothing as I moved away. In this manner, I could spiral into a more exact location and size of the phone. Pinpointing the sound. The sound corresponded to lights on the display. "So, bombies sound a certain way?"

"Yes, we can tell the difference between a bombie and a grenade based on the sound."

"Do detectors all sound the same?"

"Yes, it is some kind of international standard. Everywhere we go, the bombs will all sound the same. But out here, with lots of birds and wind, it can be hard to hear."

I handed the detector back to Vanida, who readjusted the length for her much shorter height.

"What does a bomb sound like?" I was thinking about the explosion in my dream that had been silenced by my waking mind, and I realized I was still listening, listening.

"I hear a sound with a long length. I go over it evenly and slowly. At a site like this, a piece of metal the size of my finger, like that artillery bullet, buried at five centimeters will signal a five, plus five lights. If that piece of metal were at twenty-five centimeters, it would not have any sound at all. I have to be familiar with the field, the soil. From checking other items, I can tell what the sound might be for this strike. This is my village, but now I hear it differently. Even with my eyes closed, I know these bombs by their sound."

My memories and fieldnotes of Vanida's village are silent as if suffering the temporary deafness experienced after an explosion. The only sound that I remember is Vanida's voice.

I knelt at the edge of the rice paddy, now clear of bombs, flooded and dotted with bundles of seedlings ready to be planted. The sky overhead glowed white, clouds wrung dry—it hadn't rained in days. All that force, now here, flowing in the dikes and paddies.

Trapped in the field, the monsoon's texture was waiting to be solid like concrete that had not yet set. Its composition was sometimes unfiltered coffee, granular; sometimes wet mortar, made of buffalo's shit and grass; and sometimes poured paint, pigmented cinnamon, rust, red ochre, orange umber, Dutch chocolate, or sepia red. The particles of clay and soil were so rich that when rubbed over my palm, they sparkled. I submerged my hand in the water of the paddy, shaking off the mud. My hand emerged gently painted with rusty rivulets, looking soft and polished.

"Look here: these new shoots." Vanida, a few steps ahead of me in the field, held up a bundle of rice seedlings dripping grainy, glutinous mud. She was smiling, proud. At their tips, the seedlings were a luscious yellow-green, the leaves straight and pointed. She gently slid her fingers down a few stalks, wiping off chunks of mud that plopped back into the muck. Revealed at their base, the green paled to a white, slender bulb bearded with orange roots. "This is rice; this is life. Planted in safe ground."

In the wet season, when the rains made explosives clearance impossible, Vanida was a farmer. She wore no makeup today and no gold bracelet.

"We are the people that didn't leave during the war." More than a quarter of Laos' population fled as war refugees during the nine years of the American bombing. Many of those people never returned. "But, because we stayed, we had to learn to accept the war into our lives. A lot of the bombs are in the rice paddies, which is also where we must grow our rice to feed ourselves. We have to do this, even if the ground is contaminated. So it is good that this field is safe since our team has cleared it."

She wiped her free hand on her worn cotton sihn, already dirty.

"I know that in America you have paved roads and lawns," the way she said this implied that she knew this from photographs, "but here in Laos, we have only dirt and mud and bombs. I have studied in the city, so I know what is possible. But sometimes, when I come home for the harvest and look at my family, I think to myself: they don't know anything else! This is all they know!" She held her hands out waist-high, palms up, still proud, indicating the swollen paddy beneath her. The surface of the paddy vibrated like the skin on a drum, as if sensitive to the sound of her voice.

"This is all they know. I look at a house like this," she gestured to one of the woven huts beyond the field, "and I think: If a rich American family moved in, they could not live here. They would have too much stuff. But if this family moved to an American house, they could live there just fine. They would have everything they wanted. It is not fair that some people have what they need, and others do not."

I nodded, yes. "How does that make you feel?"

"Sad. Look, there: that woman owns no shoes." Vanida pointed to an older woman planting the far side of the paddy. Her back curved like a fishhook, feet splayed farther apart than her hips. Gray, streaked hair fell from her topknot and trailed in the water. "She is wearing all the clothes that she owns. When we are done planting today, she will wash herself with her clothes still on because she has no others to change in to. But she is smiling."

"She does not know that she is poor."

"Exactly, and because I am the daughter of the village chief, and my family owns a hotel in the city, and I studied in the city and work for a big, international organization I know that she is poor. Is it good that I know this? Sometimes I wonder if it might be better not to teach people about poverty."

One foot at a time, I stepped into the paddy. Shoeless, the warm mud closed over my feet. I sensed little unseen animals crawling under, over, between my toes. Monks stayed out of the mud, but that was a privilege these women did not have. I felt large, clotted chunks of buffalo manure crumble underfoot. The field smelled like a wet animal; I could almost feel the hot breath of the water buffalo lazing nearby. I stood still a moment to secure my footing. Thick coffee-and-milk water swirled my ankles. The water was too thick to see through. When I raised my feet, the mud split in large cuboid chunks, parting like thick pudding.

Women were out in the field, bent double, skirts tucked up between their legs or tied at their sides. Most were already mud-gray to their thighs. In Lao villages, women were the ones responsible for planting rice. There were no men here and no red warning signs. The pale-yellow circles of the women's bamboo hats bobbed up and down, arms quick into the muck and back, the motion like kingfishers hunting for snakes. I touched my bamboo hat, on loan from Vanida's mother, doubtful that I would work so quick.

The women moved together through the paddy in a horizontal line, walking backward. Holding a green bundle under one arm, with their opposite hand, they slid the seedlings into the mud between thumb and two fingers. In neat rows, each tiny seedling cast spider silk shadows over the polished surface of the field. Behind the women, bundles of new seedlings sat upright at regular intervals, like upside-down green silk tassels.

Vanida was before me in the field. Reaching down to her reflection in the water, Vanida's arms touched and then merged with her mirror image, forming a complete circuit with her legs, her bent back, and her arms. Seen reflected in the ring of her double, she clasped the sky nearly white after rain and the clouds washed clean. Smell of shit, shoeless, a little frog.

The night after my dream explosion, I left my bowl out by the sink below the open kitchen window. The rains came in the evening, pounding against the walls, and I forgot to close the window. The next morning, the monsoon had swept the counters and floors with glittering residue and filled the bowl with stormwater. Polluted, laced with black flakes, a sparkling morning offering.

8

"DO YOU KNOW HOW LAOS WORKS?" Emilia asked and then replied, without waiting for me to answer. "Let me tell you."

My answer would have been some high theory, probably a Stanley Tambiah reference, something about galactic polities and scaling power structures. Clearly, that was not the conversation Emilia was getting at: I politely listened.

She tapped her cigarette on the railing of the office patio once, twice.

"I was here three years ago—that was my first time in Laos—on a project team for a big international clearance organization. I was still a consultant. Our team was traveling around Pakse. We got lunch at this little noodle shop and I left my purse. There was nothing crucial in it, I kept my passport and such in the hotel safe, so it wasn't that important. My hotel key, some local money. That's what was in it. And we left that area so fast that I didn't go back and pick it up. I just thought: it's lost now! A donation to the local economy!"

She dragged slow on her cigarette. The tiny embers sizzled audibly. Her dyed blonde hair showed brown at the roots, pinned back, but escaping in large windblown curls. Twin gold studs in her ears. Black sunglasses with tiny silver bevels at the joints, lenses dark gray. The ashtray—her ashtray—on the patio railing was a little puddle, where floated a mash of stumps.

"But then, three years later, I'm sitting in a café in Vientiane. The owner of the café comes up to me and says, 'Ma'am, is this yours?' And it's my purse! Everything was in it, even the money. I've never seen this person before in my life. He says that he got it from his sister, who got it from a friend, who got it from a relative, et cetera et cetera, who owns a noodle shop in a little village outside Pakse. Vientiane is nowhere near Pakse. They'd been passing around my description for three years, asking people to look out for a survey consultant from South Africa missing a purse."

She sat back, as though she'd made her point. "That's how Laos works."

"Hey, anthropologist, did you bring your camera?" Emilia asked from the front passenger seat. "This village is beautiful. It's very remote—no markets, no foreign stuff of any kind. They still live very authentically."

Next to her, Channarong was driving the jeep with single-minded concentration. A lot of humanitarian organizations hired specialized drivers to ferry foreign staff from place to place. Foreigners were discouraged from driving or obtaining Lao drivers' licenses, but I'd only seen this enforced in the capital city. I didn't have a license and no one in Laos bothered to check if I had one: being white, the assumption was that I would be driven by others. I never asked Channarong if he had permission to drive. I supposed that since he was a Thai citizen he wasn't worried about being pulled over. He drove with bluster and visible satisfaction, as if these unruly roads were a sports field or an obstacle course.

Emilia turned to face the two of us in the back: Vanida, acting as their Khmu translator, and myself, their anthropologist. She quirked a smile.

"Yes, I did bring my camera." I replied in a neutral voice. I evaded Emilia's glance and looked out the window.

I was discomforted by her elitism, yet I recognized that there were commonalities in our methods. Emilia and I were both doing cultural analysis, she as a consultant and myself as an anthropologist. Emilia had a degree in land management and was consulting with Channarong on a study of land use in this valley. I recognized at the root of her work a sincere desire to use her expertise to help others, based on shared values of repair and restitution after war—values that, to some degree, were shared between myself, the villagers of the valley, the donors, and Emilia and the other clearance staff. Beyond these shared values, each stakeholder differed in their cultural assumptions about the goals of clearance and the best use of land and resources. I consoled myself that I was more able than most to recognize my own assumptions. I believed that Emilia's flaw was to assume that these shared values equated to shared meanings: what progress meant, and for whom, and how to measure it. I tried to imagine what she meant by authenticity: How did she visit a village and decide that one was authentic and another not?

The forest out the window was a fertile backdrop for my reflections. The jungle pressed close to the jeep—I could have reached out and touched the trees—and, seen at this nearness and speed, its green boughs swept by in long lashes of color, as if by paintbrush. I imagined the bombing raids over the valley, every eight minutes for nine years. The bombs were still out there. That lingering war contamination was partly why this area had "no markets, no foreign stuff of any kind." It was too dangerous to build good roads, even if there had been money for it. And so the valley had been largely left alone. These villages were "authentic" because they were dangerous and impoverished. Emilia was right; there was something compelling about these villages. That was the irony that pulled at me from within her privileged opinions: somehow, in these villages isolated for decades by war, explosives had become part of "authentic" village life.

Emilia was wearing her signature dark sunglasses above her newly issued navy blue jumpsuit, fresh from its plastic package. Hers had deep creases at the elbows, shoulders, and running down the length of each sleeve. Her cuffs were pinched, crisp ovals around her thin wrists. One long zipper from the navel to the neck, a hand's width undone, revealed her white undershirt. In contrast, I noticed that Vanida's jumpsuit was sun-faded from hanging on the laundry line at the house she shared with the other female staff. Pale patches, cut-outs from acid-washed blue jeans, were sewn at her knees. Channarong's jumpsuit was ironed with military precision; he only wore his blues for special occasions. I assumed he had ironed it himself that morning, per worn-out orders from his tour in Afghanistan.

I looked out of place in my long-sleeved pink linen shirt, jeans, and closed-toe sandals. Everyone else in the car was wearing regulation jumpsuits and black army boots. My hiking sandals were pushing the line—it's not like I was actually blowing up bombs or anything. But I regretted the pink shirt: it was the last clean one in my luggage, and I put it on with a bit of dread imagining what Channarong would say about my wearing pink. A bright, Schiaparelli shocking pink. Sure enough, as I stepped up to open the jeep's door that morning, he had looked me up and down and drawled, "No one's ever worn pink to one of my clearance sites before." I had huffed: "I don't recall regulations saying what color I could wear." I was upset at him for being sexist.

Emilia, oblivious to my meditations, said cryptically: "We need to get them to walk the polygon."

She opened her mouth to continue briefing—then shut it when the car jolted over a large, cracked ridge of dried mud. The road was its own incredible terrain, nearly unnavigable but for Channarong's expert driving. The mud of this road had been carved by the heavy jeeps and trucks of the explosives clearance teams working the area. Now the rain had stopped, and the mud had dried into narrow wheel-wide tracks and deep, sloping depressions. Conversation followed the shape of the road when the way was smooth.

I learned that Emilia's "polygon" was a recently cleared airstrike, so-called because of the typical shape of strike zones on clearance maps. Channarong trained his team to walk their metal detectors in straight lines; this manner of walking an area produced clearance maps composed of "lanes" and "turning points" which together created a polygon. Airstrikes are not made up of straight lines or corners, but it is more efficient to clear a strike shaped that way. This particular polygon had a border of about two miles, following the edge of the main road, the turns of banana fields, and, at places, cutting lanes through the semi-cultivated jungle. Today, Emilia and Channarong planned to present a map of the completed clearance project to village residents. They would walk the residents around the border of the newly cleared area, literally "walking the polygon" marked in red on the map.

The car windows were all rolled down to bring the cool driving air into the vehicle. The only time we were truly cool—when the windows were down, driving fast. Dirt came in, too, covering my linen shirt in delicate orange ochre—like fuzz, until I touched it and the sweat on my hands made it paint.

There were few other people on the road. A boy bumped past us on a motorbike, walking his vehicle over a steep rut, where we also paused, and waved his right of way to cross before us. The tired boy was painted head to toe in orange dust except for two spots at his temples where the sweat had washed him like a benediction. He passed down my side of the vehicle, and we briefly made eye contact: brown eyes, even his lashes were dusted orange.

"We've yet to find an actual landowner here," Emilia continued, pacing her words around potholes, holding steady to the headrest. "They don't have property rights in land in this village—it is all owned in a seasonal rotation of who is cultivating what. But I can't get people to answer my questions about how it works."

I understood her frustration. Explosives technicians rely on landowners who can take responsibility for facilitating clearance and can later be counted as beneficiaries in reports to donors. A village without property rights in land is a serious obstacle to proper procedure. Copies of documents relating to clearance, such as land title documents and certificates of clearance, were intended to be shared with the village chief for safekeeping. The chief in this village had no such stored documents—and very little interest in Emilia's "procedure." As a result, Emilia was behind schedule: it had taken her three weeks to get the chief to stamp her reports. Red stamps were fetishes for development workers, in the sociological sense. At planning meetings, she talked as if the stamp were a person who approved, rather than a tool of the chief: "We can't move forward until we get the stamp." These discussions sometimes eclipsed, or shadowed, the very real people that offered or withheld approval. Within the village, withholding a stamp was one of the few ways that the chief could forestall or withhold consent for a project. A pink rubber stamp with a short, polished wooden handle, damp and wrapped in a plastic bag together with a small container of moldy red ink.

We passed the jeep of another clearance team traveling in the opposite direction. Identical white cars, though theirs was dirtier. The two jeeps exchanged friendly honks.

"We have to educate the villagers about clearance," Emilia continued. "Because the assumption is that everywhere is dangerous. They think that if we don't clear it, then it is still contaminated. We need to make sure that they understand that the cleared area is safe *and* the uncleared area is safe. They need to understand that there is no evidence of contamination outside the cleared area—that's why we didn't clear it!"

This village had only recently become accessible by car, and then only reachable during the dry season when the rivers receded to reveal low concrete bridges crossing their rocky beds. The rivers ran fast and clear, cutting deep gorges in the high mountains around us. The dirt road was never flat, but always rolling down to a river or climbing up from a river. We crossed a half-dozen at least on our way to this village, each the same cold water, the same rippling skin moving fast, the same pale stones glimmering beneath. Even during the dry season, the concrete bridges were always partially submerged, stained with the dark ink of the water. Training for bomb technicians included an advanced course in off-road driving.

Channarong had traveled these roads for the last several months since the valley opened to car traffic. He was rigid in the driver's seat, leaning forward slightly, chin out, and hardly spoke a word. With his hands at ten and two, he slid the wheel through his fingers like a rope pulled taut. Sitting behind him in the rear seat, I noticed that the collar of his jumpsuit was stained with sweat.

With palpable relief, Channarong pulled the jeep into a sloping open field and parked below a small, white concrete schoolhouse surrounded by a waist-high fence of faded blue slats. The car sighed into a stop.

Turning off the car engine uncovered the softer sounds of chickens squawking at each other, wooden bells chiming from the necks of water buffalo—no humans in sight. There was a shared silence while our bodies enjoyed being still.

"We found eighty-eight cluster bomblets in that schoolyard," Channarong said and pointed through the windshield.

Emilia pulled her sunglasses down her nose to make eye contact with Vanida and me in the backseat. She looked at us over her black rims, eyebrows raised. "Are we ready?"

Ready for what?

The car door snapped shut behind her.

The whole village was sideways, life on a slope. Above, the sharp, pale peaks of the mountain ridge cut into teeth by many rivers; below, the dense green mosaics of the tree canopy. Partway between was the village, about ten well-kept houses with freshly woven bamboo thatch walls and roofs. Houses were arranged descending a path that zigzagged the mountain slope, with the schoolhouse at the highest level, parallel to the road. Three levels below us, bright patches of yellow and orange where blankets were laid out to dry over a fence.

I heard a wind chime—turned, saw that the chime hanging from the corner of the schoolhouse roof was made from the hollowed hemispheres of cluster submunitions.

Channarong had also noticed the wind chime. He winked at me. "At least we know we're in the right place."

No one came out to meet us.

Sounds of distant laughter, then, abruptly, the high whine of a radio being tuned, out of range, turned off. More silence.

Emilia and Vanida walked the village looking for the chief, while Channarong began setting up his map presentation. He pinned the clearance map to a poster board set on a large easel in the schoolyard. He did not look left or right, just at the work in front of him, taking his time, each slow motion an invitation for residents to notice and come over.

"We found 670 explosive items in this village, including 524 cluster submunitions and 81 cannon rounds. All this on a total of 159 square meters. That's four items per square meter. No one had come here before; we're the first clearance team to work in this area. We were here even before the road was built."

"Are you going to just give your presentation to me, then?"

He chuckled. "Maybe. You're studying this, after all. Also, you're the only one here."

He carefully secured the handover paperwork under a nearby rock so it didn't blow away.

"Before the road was built, we sent a team here with donkeys carrying our gear as part of an emergency clearance project." He paused to look at me. "Donkeys don't work for most clearance projects—it's too hard to carry equipment, and you have to bring along food for the donkeys—but there was a huge mother bomb near the main water source for all the villages in this valley. Nearly 300 cluster submunitions were released from that one bomb, scattered around the water pump. We only had the funding to clear that one strike directly around the pump. So now the pump was clear. But all around it, where the people walk to the pump, what about that? Everyone knew that the rest of the valley was unsafe. It didn't make any sense—but clearance takes money."

"So now you are back to finish the job?"

"Yeah, to do it properly."

Channarong gestured uphill, beyond the schoolhouse. "The cluster strike begins uphill and runs off into the jungle." He paused and playfully nodded to my pink shirt. "I won't ask a lady to come out and look at that part—it's a mess."

Taken aback, I didn't say anything. The two of us had traipsed through thornier bushes before; why was he treated me different now that I was wearing pink?

Turning back to the map, Channarong pointed out the corresponding locations. The red dots coalesced in thick swirls, almost patterned, but somehow elusive. The strike didn't seem to have any edges—there was no part of the map that wasn't marked with at least one dot. Each dot was a bomb or bomb fragment, dug up and destroyed. The pilots had probably been targeting this village on the assumption that the villagers were allied with the guerrilla revolutionaries up north. They had bombed this valley every day for nine years. At that level of intensity, their goal would not have been to merely destroy the villages but also to terrorize the valley inhabitants. Air warfare is a type of terrorism. The ground, the gardens and rice fields, the sky, the daylight—under an air war, these essential things each became a way to die. Bombings layered on top of each other in Channarong's clearance map. I couldn't identify the oval footprints of individual strikes.

"Emilia says they're not planning on using that land in the next five years, so we cut off the polygon here—" He indicated a sharp diagonal line on the map. "And didn't clear past this line. That means that we didn't clear everything in the village vicinity, and we need to make sure the landowners and the chief know that. We really would prefer not to go off chasing bombs into the jungle if there is no point!"

"Did you check to see if the village uses that jungle for foraging? Even if it is not in the five-year plan . . ." I thought of Emilia's comment in the car about the village being safe. Technically, perhaps this was true, but only under the assumption that the villagers never foraged for wild foods.

He shrugged, frowning. "We can't clear everything. Some of that is just jungle. We don't have the time or money to clear anything that isn't in the village development plan. That's why they need to know what's safe and what's not."

I settled back on my heels, silent and unsure of myself. What was my role in this, as an anthropologist—and unfortunately this mattered—wearing pink? Did my role include pushing Channarong to imagine the way that the locals saw their village, their needs and goals?

Emilia and Vanida approached from uphill, two older men behind them. One—the chief, I assumed—was carrying a little plastic bag. The chief's stamp. The other dragged a few steps behind, shuffling, his feet scuffing the dirt in a series of orange puffs.

Emilia pointed behind her to the first man. "The chief."

He waved a little; said nothing. He didn't offer his name, and Emilia didn't either.

And she pointed to the second man. "He says he's the landowner."

She approached us and lowered her voice. "This isn't one of the people I did the land survey with. I've never seen him before."

Channarong didn't say anything, looking unsure.

"Well, we cannot just leave! This guy," she gestured with her chin toward the supposed landowner, "must come with us or it's just pointless. We must walk the polygon with the landowner and the village chief. And he says he'll walk it with us."

The two men looked to be in their late fifties, which meant that they'd survived these airstrikes.

Vanida and I exchanged a doubtful glance. Translator and anthropologist, our roles were somewhat ambiguous, there to observe and help if asked. It was a bit like watching friends disrespect the hosts at a dinner party. I thought again about authenticity, safety, and danger; the way that clearance made things safe by imposing a Western social order that was not the order familiar to these villagers. Emilia's paperwork misrepresented the way that people lived on this land, but Emilia couldn't officially release the land as cleared until she got the proper stamps. It was a mismatch peculiar to Western staff: the assumption that paperwork could be made to match reality, and where the two misaligned, the world of the paperwork imposed itself on the world of the real. Paper villages and paper landowners and paper chiefs. People made of bleached-white paper and musty red ink: a poor map of human meaning.

The chief looked at the map with reserved interest. From his shirt pocket, he removed a pair of battered gold reading glasses, unfolded the wireframe, and looped the temples over his ears. Bespectacled, he leaned toward the map, reading the Lao language key in the lower left. Lao was almost certainly not his first language—his native language was probably a dialect of Khmu, the language of this part of the valley. Often, chiefs were the only Lao-literate members of a village. The central government required chiefs to be proficient in spoken and written Lao and to have obtained a minimum public education.

Channarong started to describe the map's features to him—the red dots, the border. The chief listened to Channarong's description and Vanida's Khmu translation with a politician's vacant attention, polite but disengaged. His eyes lingered over the red border. When Vanida finished, the chief pointed at the sharp diagonal line marking the longest edge of the polygon, and asked in Lao rather than Khmu: "You only cleared this area?"

Vanida answered the chief, without bothering to translate for Emilia: "Yes, just this area. Because past that line, this land isn't in your five-year plan."

The chief nodded. He knew the clearance team hadn't cleared the whole strike. The first clearance team came to this area four months ago, forty years after the war ended. But for decades before that, without assistance from beyond the valley, villagers had been clearing their land, dismantling the bombs as they were able. The wind-chime was evidence. Lost in his thoughts, the chief sighed and traced the border of the polygon with his fingers, smoothing the wrinkled paper. Turning away from the map, he removed his reading glasses and patted their frame into his shirt pocket.

We began walking to the nearest turning point of the polygon, accessible via the main dirt road that ran through and past the village. Emilia stopped periodically to show the village chief and landowner where we were on the map. The group headed to the banana fields and farms uphill of the school. The monsoon rains had been sweeping the bombs downhill, into the village, for decades.

After a half-mile of walking, we veered off the main road and down a small footpath. The trees in this area were quite young: slim trunks patterned by thin vines. The shade enveloped us. It was much cooler under the trees. Behind me, I heard the small noises of the chief and the landowner following us deeper into the clearance zone. Bushes pressed aside, the footstep crinkle of dry leaves. *Whap whap* of the chief's plastic bag with the stamp, held tight in his fist, hitting his thigh as he walked.

We marched single file down the footpath until Channarong found two tall red stakes about two meters off the path—this was the first turning point in the polygon. He stood next to the stakes and said in slow and careful Lao: "This is the boundary. On this side," he pointed, "we cleared. On this side," he pointed the other way, "we didn't. Understand?"

The chief nodded without waiting for Vanida's Khmu translation, then said curtly in Lao: "Yes, I understand."

The chief had chosen to speak in a less familiar language and refused Vanida's translation. He refused to explain how residents managed their land, or to respond to the team's bureaucratic requirements. My sense was that he didn't want to be understood by the team, of which I was nominally a member. I saw his noncompliance as a form of civil disobedience: his refusal to become understand-able, and therefore categorized and ranked, by these foreigners. And his noncompliance formed a pair with Emilia and Chann-arong's persistent cultural ignorance, their refusal to understand the unique people of the village. The team's map and five-year plan as-sumed Western social norms like land ownership and markets—it was easier for Channarong to assume the map was accurate rather than to question what things were on the map or left off entirely. In Emilia's paperwork, every chief, every landowner, and every vil-lage was somewhat replaceable: if one landowner went missing, then she found another one, and it didn't matter much that none of them were real. I felt a humbling, belittling sense of finding a small dot in a global conflict of culture that extended out beyond these red lines.

There is a popular entertainment in Laos based on shadow pup-petry: large, intricately cut and cleverly articulated figures are held up against a white screen, lit from behind. The effect from the front is lively: the lithe shadows of animals and people and gods jump, sing, and dance. Once, I tiptoed around and lifted the curtain on the back of the performers' truck: from behind, I saw a lamp attached to a genera-tor; a pile of slack flat figures, eyes without light; a young dark-haired apprentice with a basket of clappers, bells, and thunder-sticks; and a whiskered small old man smoking a joint. The magic continued, the lover saved, the monster slayed, but seen from the back the story be-came unbelievable.

I think this is a little bit like what the chief found when he looked behind the curtain of humanitarian clearance: shadows and trickery, and the thin façade of a safe village. The figures on the screen were warped versions of real villages and real people, stereotypes with huge shadows. All other things being unequal between them, the chief refused to be typecast.

The jungle on either side of the staked line looked identical: thinly leafed carpet, dappled shadows, large black butterflies moving in and out of the shadows, moving like shadows across the invisible boundary. The group returned to the footpath and continued to walk the polygon—led by Emilia, map in hand, then Channarong and Vanida, then myself, and finally the chief and landowner following last. There was no conversation, not even the chatter of birds. All the birds had been trapped and eaten. When we reached the next turning point of the polygon, the chief and landowner disappeared into the dappled shadows. Emilia turned around, beginning to point out this next landmark, and found them both—gone.

9

IN THE STORAGE SHED beneath Bounmi's stilt house, what I first took to be sheaves of grain turned out to be dusty lengths of helicopter artillery cartridges, powdered pale beige with age, and beneath them, cardboard boxes of cluster submunitions neatly packed like winter apples. He called it his "personal cache" for home use: mostly metal repair, sometimes he used the bombs for fishing, sometimes demolitions to remove trees from a field. The men of the village, he said, kept their larger bombs in a "secret cache" in the jungle safe from the prying eyes of the clearance officers who were trained to demolish all bombs on sight.

What I first took to be a fence along the south wall of the pasture turned out to be rusting sheets of a dismantled airplane, relics from the war. The plane had gone down near the village and Bounmi's father had saved the wreckage for memory. The carved wooden poles of his house turned out to be the fins of submerged general-purpose bombs, used as plinths for the foundations; and the buffalo pond, a crater.

What I first took to be accidents turned out to be intentional casualties of a war calculated to weaken the Lao state if it went communist. Not peace, but a fragment of war, half-buried and dangerous.

What I first took, I could not give back, and so I walked through Bounmi's farm seeing double. And then, in the trash pile behind Bounmi's house, what I first took to be a discarded fragment of a bomb turned out to be part of a motorcycle engine. Metal was so rare in these villages, even a small piece caught my eye. A crescent of tarnished silver, the length of my flat hand, two screw holes at either end indicating that it was half of a pair. I picked it up, weighed in my palm. I puzzled over it; the metal was too fresh and still slightly oiled. Not a bomb fragment. Sometimes, metal scraps were pieces of livelihood. And yet, I pocketed it as a reminder that this old war tended to overshadow everyday life. Like blinking away an afterimage—what I saw contrasted with the bright shadows of things that weren't there anymore.

I followed the war scrap trader up the ladder into the single room of his small thatch house. It had been two weeks since I first met Bounmi at his exorcism. His house had only one wall and, but for a short railing, was open to the cool wind on three sides. The house was a kind of elevated pavilion. Tall spikes of papaya grew by the railing, an easy harvest from Bounmi's sleeping mat. Two cups and a pot of mulberry tea were set on a small plastic tray on a three-legged stool, waiting for us to sit down.

Green geckos grow big as cats in the high eaves, chirping above us. "This area was part of a mercenary camp. There are big bombs still here, too deep to clear, behind this house," Bounmi said by way of welcome, in English. "When I built this house, there was a crater behind this building from two accidents, two people died. Just over there," he said and pointed to the trash pit, a crater after all.

"So there are bombs under the house?"

"Yes . . . very big bombs. I dug down to look at them, but I don't know how to clear them, so I buried them again. They are still there."

His body had an electric energy, like a coiled battery, that I have seen before in the very young and that quivered to the tips of his rough-shorn hair. I imagined he was charged with the electricity of unspent youth. Bounmi spoke in fast, quick sentences—there was a feeling of show-and-tell, the way a boy shows his treasures to his mates. Again, I was reminded that he was far younger than he looked. The heavy cloak was gone from him—I had not seen its shadow since the exorcism—but he still carried a dark presence, no longer oppressive. He was dressed in what I took to be his grandfather's old army shirt. Bounmi poured the tea into our twin China-blue cups.

"Did you try to move to another part of the land?"

He huffed a half-laugh. "They are under everyone's house. There's nowhere to move."

I followed his gaze to a low shelf running around the length of the room, attached to the railing, displaying defused cluster submunitions set in wood cases like delicate Fabergé eggs.

"This stuff, it has a meaning because I found it on our land, on our parents' land." He pointed in turn to different bombs displayed around him: "This one is American, this one is Russian, this one is Chinese. I have more outside."

This was somehow funnier, and he let out a full-belly cackle. "This is my bomb garden, where I grow bombs. Because America dropped them in the soil, and now they grow, you see?"

Bounmi had given himself the job of repurposing bombs for things other than war: cookpots, fence posts, cow troughs, boats, and also jokes. It was a common joke in the valley, that the bombs were seeds growing underground or fruit ripening on trees. It was a horrible joke, disconcertingly gentle, and I had heard it elicit a kind of mournful laughter, a salvage humor sewn together from scraps of violence. I didn't find these jokes funny, but I also didn't grow up in the valley. People most often encountered bombs in their orchards, rice paddies, and farms, where they were much like seeds—when the bombs go off, they reap their own harvest.

In America, nuclear weapons experts named the first atomic bombs using words for a family: they said *fat man* and *little boy*. A grizzled American bomb technician once told me that an unopened cluster munition was a *pregnant mother*. In my native California, my family talked about bombs in a language that mixed military slang with Hollywood tropes: Dad said of a news report from the Middle East that an explosion was a *blockbuster* and *that was like the scene in* Die Hard. We compared our bombs to other bombs, and our violence to other violence real or imagined. I remember reading accounts of the American Civil War in which volunteer farmers-turned-soldiers referred to powder explosions—an ancient precursor to modern dynamite, far less powerful, and probably the first bombs these soldiers had experienced in their lives—as *tornadoes*, or if heard from a distance *the wind in a wheat field, the buzzing of a hive of bees*, and other farmstead phrases. I thought about the many ways that war violence becomes part of our everyday experience, named and known. In Laos, where most people are farmers, they also used farming metaphors to name their bombs.

"What kind of bombs do you find in this area?"

"There was not only bombing, but also ground-fighting. So I find a lot of Russian artillery. Bullets and metal helmets. There are always lots of cluster bombs where the Americans came. I have to learn this history by myself, because people don't talk about it, but it is hidden all around me. Even the official clearance teams only have shallow knowledge about the bombs they find: the type of ordnance, how to blow it up. They don't know who made it, who sold it, where it is from, or why it was dropped here. They don't know that Americans bombed us for nine years. Their education is not so deep."

"You know these bombs better than they do," I suggested.

He nodded. "Because bombs are part of my life."

"What do you mean?"

"Because bombs are in our land and they have killed my friends and family already. Everything I do, I have to do with bombs first. It's quite hard to do farming, or make a fire, because I have to know what is underneath." Bounmi patted the floor; the floorboards were not flush and through the slits I could see the gray-dusty ground beneath me. The sun was two hours past zenith, and light came in on every side of the house: in long flashes up through the floorboards, needling white rays through the house's one wall so that the bamboo weave appeared to sparkle, shimmering patches through the thatch roof, and in soft shining rectangles draping the west-facing railings. Three-fourths in shadow, Bounmi was crouching under the camouflage of leaves.

"Help me understand: How would you make a fire?"

"I would use a hoe instead of a shovel, because a hoe is more gentle. I would dig slowly, thirty centimeters down and check the soil with my hands. If it is clear, then I would make a fire there. Sometimes it is quite hard to be properly safe. We do slash-and-burn farming, and we can't check all the fields first for bombs. So we start the fire two or three kilometers away, in the most far away field, and then we see what happens. If we find something, we have to run very fast!"

Sitting cross-legged, he rubbed his palms on his knees in a way that conveyed satisfaction. He smiled, energized by the memory. "Anything you need to do, you need to do with bombs first. That is why bombs are part of life."

Then he rocked back on his hips, thinking, with his head down.

"Also, we can use them to make our living," he continued in his fast voice. He was pointing at the relics in his bomb garden. "There is little to sell in this village. If we want cash, we have to sell something in the market. Bombs are part of our livelihood, our entertainment and our protection. Selling bombs is the easiest way to get cash because we have nothing else to sell. In the market, buyers come from all over—I sell to Vietnamese, to Chinese, to Malaysian buyers. So my bombs go all over the world—I think some of them make it back to America!" He slapped his thighs and rocked back on his hips, chuckling. "We are a small village, but the bombs connect us to the big world. Sometimes, the American POW teams come here and hire me to help them find bones of dead Americans. I find many bombs that way, too. This is how we make money. Bombs are part of our daily use because there are a lot in the village and we have to use something, so we make them the stilts of our houses, our fences. It is not meaningful anymore, it is just part of life. I could use bombs for anything."

He hesitated before adding, "Some people use mines as protection from robbers or any kind of people they don't think are good. They use the leftovers from the war to save our lives today. Mountain tribes, rebels. Rebels come down from the mountains to steal our food . . . it is kind of like a civil war using the weapons of another war. These are the weapons we have. The clearance teams don't know that we do this. We did it this way, by moving the old landmines so that they are between us and the mountains. The old bombs are still used."

"What else could you use bombs for?" I hesitated to even ask.

"You must understand," he said and raised his hands out flat and even as a balanced scale. One hand was in sunlight. First, he lowered his right hand, "I could go to the market and buy a knife, or," and then he lifted his left hand, "I could dismantle a bomb and use the metal to make a knife in the blacksmith in the ban. Cheaper."

Bounmi must have sensed my uncertainty—I had trouble understanding him because I was simultaneously trying to understand something about my own life back in California. *That was a blockbuster. Just like the scene in* Die Hard. Something about Bounmi's repurposing of bombs, making them into things no less violent but somehow less recognizably warlike, was helping me to understand my own pragmatic familiarity with war: I remembered that my local police force had recently acquired a small fleet of secondhand armored army vehicles, mine-resistant and able to withstand explosives, but repainted black and white for our city streets. I sensed the war disappearing into the larger pattern, as the individual weft threads disappear under the motion of a shuttle loom. Large social forces spun patterns through our lives, obscuring violence in the weave. The whole thing reminded me of Geertz's description of human culture as spiders spinning webs: "Man is an animal suspended in webs of significance he himself has spun." We were like two spiders in our separate webs. Bounmi must consciously and with great effort hang each insulating thread, spinning himself meaning.

"You see this?" He pointed to the fields beyond the railing. "I have a farm next to my house, so I want to look deeper for bombs before I plant. My family land is twenty-three hectares, mostly we can't use it due to the bombs. Finally, since I started working on this about four months ago, I have cleared two hectares. I don't go every day; let's say twice a week. About twenty bombs on my two hectares."

"How do you clear your land?" Every battlefield was also a house, a pasture, or a farm.

"The best way is to look for them on the surface. That is the first way to look. The second way is with a metal detector: we have cheap detectors from Vietnam so we can use that to look underground. It is cheap tech, but it works. The third way is with a hoe and by hand, digging. I learned this way from my grandfather, who was a soldier in the Lao People's Army during the war. He had to clear many, many bombs."

"So your grandfather taught you?"

"Not at first. I learned from other children. Playing with bombs is common for us. That's how I learned first: I was not educated about them in school, so I didn't know what they were when I found them in the forest. My friends and I would throw them around, these cluster bombs, because we didn't know. Some kids even did slingshots to shoot the bombies. I was lucky."

"Later, my grandfather and my father taught me," he pointed again to the ordnance in his collection, "that this is a bomb, this is a bomb, this is a bomb. My father took me out into the woods and taught me how to identify them. He took a cluster munition and said, 'This is a BLU-26' and then set it on fire . . . *boom!* That is how I learned that they explode. What we learn, we learn from our parents and our neighbors. I learned that they explode, but I didn't know how they worked. Many people don't understand yet how dangerous this is, because the only way to really learn is by showing an explosion. People do not know how dangerous their own life is here. After I saw my first explosion, I didn't leave my home for three months. But if I think like that, I won't be able to clear these bombs. Instead, I think to myself: if I clear these bombs, I stop one or two people dying."

I felt his eyes on me like cat's in the dark. I kept his gaze in mine, unblinking.

"Of course, I am scared of bombs. If you ask me 'Are you scared?' then I say, 'Yes, but I must do it: because of my unborn son.' I don't want my future son, my future wife, to be afraid. This is the way that I talk to myself. Before, when I was a child, I was scared. But if I am a scared adult, I can't take a bomb out of the ground."

"Do you have a family now?"

"No, because who would make a family in a village like this?" He gestured to his one-room house and the fruit trees beyond the railing, his bomb garden, the contaminated hectares. "What kind of life is this if I do nothing to make them safer? Each time I take a bomb out of ground, I imagine my son being born. In a future country that is safer, I am a father."

"It's going to take a long time to clear the whole country. Do you think you'll create your safe family within your lifetime?"

Bounmi was of an age to already have a wife and children.

"I don't know. Maybe not this lifetime. I imagine my son and how I want him to live. I don't want him to be afraid and have to worry about what is underneath the ground. I can feel in my blood how long it will take to clear this country, and I know that I will be dead before this is over. Now, instead of fear, I imagine my son being the next person to continue what I am doing."

"Just like you inherited this from your father, and before him, your grandfather."

He nodded, closing his eyes, and I felt let go, like a hand loosening. I couldn't remember the last time I saw Bounmi blink.

"I tried to apply to be a clearance technician in the provincial capital. I walked in with my application and handed it to the secretary. She knew me and did not looked at it, told me that they don't hire cowards who work the black market. She just put it in the trash and told me not to come back."

There was one printer in the village, available for rent at a small internet café owned by the village chief. Bounmi had paid to have his application printed, and then traveled the six-hours round-trip to the city and back. She knew him. Did he mean that she knew he was upland Hmong, or knew that he was a scrap trader? Clearance officers and scrap traders worked the same areas—they were practically work colleagues—and often knew each other well. Did the secretary recognize him by his accent, his clothing, his reputation? I guessed it didn't matter, because Bounmi was sure she was never going to give him a chance at the job.

"The secretary, she was lowland Lao. All the jobs in the city are for lowland Lao." Many upland Hmong had fought for the American-backed royalists during the Secret War, against the communist revolutionaries that are now in charge, and the current government still sometimes treated the Hmong as rebels less deserving of jobs and social services. Many upland groups, especially the Hmong, fled persecution in Laos after the revolution and settled in farming communities throughout California's Central Valley and the plains of the American Midwest. But some upland groups, including Bounmi's family, had fought on the side of the communists.

The Lao government measures race by altitude, not skin color: the higher up the mountains, the less civilized and less able to develop. It is part of the power of racism to appear natural—and in Laos, that nature lies along the slant of a mountain. Race, whether in Laos or in America, is a way of defining social inequality and not intrinsic natural differences. Historically, the mountains have been places of refuge from the Lao state, zones of relative autonomy and freedom for the groups that lived on these sky-high steppes and slopes. In the early stages of the Secret War, these mountains hosted both the communist revolutionaries and the CIA's secret training camps. Under the influence of French administrators, the royal regime simplified Lao race to just three types (highlanders, midlanders, and lowlanders) and gave each type an altitude quotient. Three is a lucky number in Lao Buddhism (believers take refuge in the Buddha, the Dharma, and the Sangha) and an enduring symbol of unity in Lao politics. Today in Laos, people are still officially divided into three altitude types and then often further subdivided by dialect or cultural group such as Lao, Hmong, Mon-Khmer, Khmu, or Ahka. At the morning market, when Vanida told me that upland foods were for poor people, she was speaking this altitude racism.

Roughly a third of the population is lowland ethnic Lao. The lowland elites, in their river cities, assumed themselves to be superior and more suited to rule. Midlanders and highlanders are sometimes pejoratively referred to as khaa, *slaves,* as if they were intrinsically inferior and more suited to labor. Despite this history of racial prejudice, and supported by recent communist projects of multiethnicity, the country has an established record of working toward racial justice: civil rights were included in the first Lao constitution, nearly a decade before the American civil rights movement. While this altitude-based system of race and ethnicity predates the current regime, the categories of lowlander, midlander, and highlander are still widely used in governance. Bounmi's upland Hmong grandfather may have fought in the revolutionary army, but that history of proletariat struggle has since been supplanted by a persistent racial logic of national development sweeping from the valley up to the mountain.

"I want to work with the official teams, but they don't want to work with me! My question is: Even the people that clear these bombs today, why do they get lazy? They get lazy because it takes a long time to properly clear anything, and they have no sense of finishing it. It is a problem of clearance: the people who work this job just want a better life, a better salary. They are not thinking about the better future for everyone, just for themselves in the short-term. I don't know why they are thinking like that, but they should be happy, they should love that they are doing this, even if their life isn't better off immediately. I would like to have their job instead of them. Everyone here has a relative who is in clearance. Everyone.

"I want to start a clearance team of my own, very official, and not in the black market like my scrap trading. We scrap traders are small fish in the stream. My dream is that I have an official team of local experts and educated people from abroad. The government would get funding to buy us equipment . . . I think my team would be more successful than the foreign teams. People here had to learn to clear their own land, for many decades, before the foreign teams came. We know our land better, we know our bombs better. Even though I don't have a sponsor right now, I have visitors and clients. I am a respected expert. I can do two jobs: farming and clearance."

"What makes you good at clearance?"

"You mean, why have I not been injured? Luck. I have stronger spirits in my body. When I was a child, Aunt Silavong looked at my hand and said that I will die of an accident. I am clumsy, I fall down all the time. I fell from the roof of the house, I fell from a mango tree. But these spirits that are in me must be stronger than my fate. I have made them even stronger by getting this tattoo." He rolled up the sleeve of his cotton shirt to show me the glowing halo of a meditating Buddha, reclining on the flank of a many-headed dragon, surrounded by Pali calligraphy. Many soldiers get tattoos as a blessing for protection, some believing that the blessings made them bullet-proof. "When I got this, maybe I was thinking of my grandfather, the soldier, who was a monk before the war. He had covered all of his body with tattoos. He was very powerful, but the bombs stilled killed him. I am human and I am not bullet-proof, so I have to be careful every step I take. I have to work and walk carefully."

He pantomimed softly walking, his hands out and fingers curled like paws.

"After I got turned down at the clearance office, I became very sick. I couldn't get out of bed: my grandfather's ghost and my father's ghost were sitting on my chest, holding me down so I couldn't breathe. I saw them in my dreams, when they told me that I must clear more bombs. Father died in an explosion—his chest was slashed, like a tiger paw." Bounmi curled his hands into claws and made the marks across his own chest. "Every night, these ghosts come to me and try to possess my body. I feel my father slipping inside me, with my breath, and holding me still; I cannot move, but I awake. I think he knows I am alone in my bed. I wake up with slashes, like my father's wounds that killed him, on my chest. I know this history is going to kill me because I cannot get all the bombs out of the ground in my lifetime. But I am smarter than these ghosts, and I learned to fall asleep with a knife under my pillow."

He held his fist up above his head, clasped tight around a knife made of air and dreams. "Ghosts were human once, and ghosts aren't very smart. They are still scared of knives!"

"The ghosts were trying to get you to clear the bombs?"

"Ghosts are only a little bit like us," he explained. "They want things, but not for the same reasons. They want to clear Laos of bombs because that is what killed them, but it is impossible, and so they would kill me for not doing the impossible. It is a kind of revenge for history."

"This is why you came to Silavong?"

"Yes, she is helping. One time when my father was still alive, I was very sick and I could not clear anything. My father hit me for not working—he said, 'You must do this work!' Very bad, my nose was bleeding. I went to Aunt Silavong, and she prayed and blew on my nose. My bleeding stopped, and she said to me, 'Now go do your father's work.'"

Bounmi's folded his arms across his chest, pretending authority. His face took on the stern, slightly sly look of Silavong, and I nearly laughed—but he wasn't trying to be funny. Behind him, a large green gecko had waddled down the wall, stopped, and slowly lifted its pointed head to look at me: vertical pupils stared over Bounmi's shoulder. Its tongue flicked out, bright pink.

"My family pushed me because if I destroy this one, or this one, I can stop one death at least. Their ghosts still push me, but it is no longer a good kind of push. I cannot clean up this entire country! I want to start my family."

I bent to refill our teacups, but the teapot was empty, only dregs.

"I have lived in this village for twenty-six years, and I just tell you what I know. I want to know what is going on here, too. I am like you: one day I will leave this place."

I put the piece of motorcycle engine in a glass jar with a canning lid and kept it sealed, like a doctors' specimen, on the shelf in my closet. Dirt settled to the bottom of the jar. Other jars were also on the shelf, and they contained: a mangled fin of a rocket, a crescent of a grenade, a hooked piece that might be the trigger of a rifle. All things that I had scavenged from my walks through battlefields.

On one of my visits, Bounmi brought out an old American guitar. Painted blue in places, but now the blue was flaking off. He said, "You are a Californian girl? I know a song for you."

There she stood in the doorway; I heard the mission bell
And I was thinking to myself
'This could be heaven or this could be hell'
Then she lit up a candle and she showed me the way
There were voices down the corridor,
I thought I heard them say
Welcome to the Hotel California

The other young men reclining in Bounmi's bomb garden began to sway and hum along with his music. There were Beer Lao cans littered in the grass. The last stragglers of a late-night party.

"I've never met a real Californian girl before," Bounmi said, "Do you have ghosts in California?"

"Yes, we do."

"Tell me about them."

I settled into a stool in the shade.

"Once, my father's partner Cybele, who is a shaman," this was almost true, though Cybele called herself a psychic, "took me and my father to a dried-up oasis, and there we found the ruins of an old town, a dried-up town, a ghost town."

The young men liked this word, *ghost town*, and I heard them whispering it in Lao: ban phi, ban phi.

"We turned down a path that led to a large, white house surrounded by palm trees. In the front of the house there was a dry, empty fountain. As I walked toward the house, I began to feel a tightness around my throat, like hands. As I get closer to the house, the tighter the hands became. I stopped walking, and just breathed, breathed, imagining loosening the hands and pushing them off. As soon as the feeling went away, I began to hear footsteps behind me in the tall, yellow grass. Those footsteps followed me into the old house, which was abandoned. I heard them following me through the rooms, up the stairs to the bedrooms, where I looked through the upper windows out to the ghost town, golden grass growing over the old roads and between the old houses. Then my father came into the room, and finally the footsteps went away and did not return. Now the house was just old and empty.

"Outside, Cybele asked me if I felt anything in the house, and I said no because I was young and did not want to admit anything. She sighed and told me that she had hoped this house was still haunted, but she didn't find any ghosts there that day. She told me that the ghost of a woman lived in the garden, and she strangled people who came to visit the house. The woman had been strangled there by a jealous lover. After she died the fountain dried up. Silently, I thought to myself: those were the hands I felt on my throat."

The young men were all looking at me, and I was proud to notice a bit of fear and admiration in their faces.

"That is a good story," one of them said. None of them asked if it was true, and it was true, and I liked that they believed me.

"We have a lot of Hmong in California," I said to the young man who had spoken. "I don't know if your ghosts can travel across the ocean to live with their relatives there."

The young man shook his head, "No, they are stuck here with us. Too many. That is why Bounmi is haunted; he has to take care of too many ghost relatives."

I glanced from the man back to Bounmi.

"Why don't they haunt him, too?"

Bounmi pointed his finger at the other man: "*His* grandfather is still alive!"

Another time, Bounmi took me to see an old American air strip out in the jungle. We hiked for two hours beyond the village, crested a hill, and saw it laid out from one end of the valley to the other. No buildings, no rusting tanks or large artillery guns. Just the black tarmac, a censor's line through a story about the slumbering shapes of hills and the embrace of strangler figs.

On my next visit, Bounmi met me at the foot of his ladder, morose and melancholy, and pressed a sheet of paper into my hands. He had no youthful energy this time; battery run down, no sparks. The shadows again circled, oval-shapes of human faces in the air, spinning like bats and, once, a bright flash as of a pair of phosphorescent eyes.

For a moment, both of our hands held the photo's four corners, then he let go.

I was holding a photo from his collection, a newspaper clipping of a thirteen-year old boy that had died in an explosion recently in the valley. I had read the news report a few days ago myself. Bounmi had printed the photo out on white paper from the village's internet café. I was slowly building an understanding of how Bounmi carried out his researches, paying per quarter-hour over a poor connection.

"This is the most recent one," he said flatly.

The boy in the photo had fallen as if still standing up: as I have seen small children fall, or recently Mali pushed over by a goat at pasture. The boy's hands were loose at his hips, his knees slightly bent and his feet evenly spaced. Like babies when napping, warm and satisfied. He fell too fast to react, in a moment of innocence that extended itself with the debris cloud, a moment that didn't settle. In the boy's tattered work pants and rucksack, blown apart, the machete's tip pointed toward the center of the explosion, I could see the outlines of what he had been doing: kneeling in the bamboo grove, using his machete to forage new shoots. Slack limbed. It is not possible to be fully prepared for a bomb; the explosion happens quicker than a human can react. Consciousness is destroyed at the center of a blast, which saves us from knowing fully what is happening. In every explosion there is something that confounds guilt or agency, where we fall over the edge of our capacity to understand. Extreme violence brings out the innocence in its victims: we are unprepared, we fall like children.

At first, I thought the photo was grayscale, but then I realized that a thin layer of explosive powder had stifled any colors. His hair was jet black. The boy's face was bloodless white—though, as I looked closer, a few small dots of blood pricked his body and the stretcher. He was lying on a stretcher of pale canvas between wooden poles, perhaps homemade, also dusted with black. The powder was a trace, a forensic trace, that marked this photograph out from other pictures of sleeping boys. The unnamed photographer had been standing above the boy, snapping the photo from directly above him. A pair of shoes, leather-laced, perhaps army boots, where visible at the lower edge of the frame. A clearance medic, documenting a case before carrying the boy into the hospital? The photo was slightly washed out, as if it had been overexposed or was a photocopy of an original.

"They are mostly boys."

I nodded, yes. "Children are now more likely to die in an explosion than their parents."

Bounmi stored his collection in a manila file-folder. Each file was carefully hand-labeled with a year, in pencil, from 1994 to the present. He had recently run out of files in the original folder and was now using tape to secure additional folders into a haphazard ac-cordion. The whole collection was wrapped in a sheet of salvaged plastic wrappers and stored in a cardboard box. Already, blotches of gray-green mold were creeping around the edges of the folders. The paper had a slightly powdery texture. In the libraries of Lao mon-asteries, monks copy books each year to preserve them from rot, but Bounmi had no helpers. My thumb and two forefingers, where I held the photo, were lightly stained gray. I wanted to ask to see his records of the three brothers' fatal scrap find, but I could not take my eyes off of this photo, this boy.

"I collect these to remind myself of what is at stake. That boy," he pointed to the photo in my hands, "could have been me, or could be my son!" His face was contorted, mouth curled up, pulled too tight. "I found many bombs in the forest when I was a boy, and I would play with them without knowing what they did until one of them killed my friend. We were alone in the forest. At first, I did not un-derstand what had happened, and once I did understand, there was nothing for me to do. That was the first time that I saw a person die."

"You watched your friend die from an explosion?" I suddenly felt the weightlessness of the photo in my hands, I felt my fingers sensitized.

"Yes, that is how I learned to fear them. I keep this collection to remind myself to be afraid."

"Is the first photo in your collection a picture of your friend?"

He nodded with his eyes closed and then opened, a little of the spark in his gaze.

"You are right: that would be the correct first photo. If I had it. But we didn't have newspapers in the ban back then. The collec-tion begins in my memory and then moves to paper. No one else is remembering this, and so each time a person dies everyone is sur-prised. In my memory and on paper, I have collected 237 deaths in this valley since I was a boy."

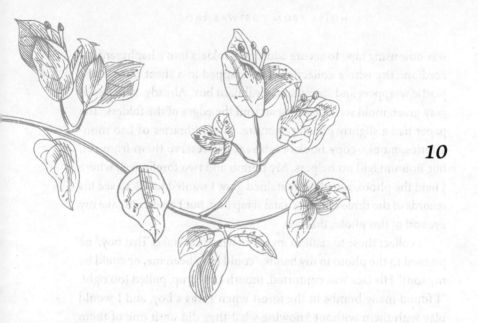

10

THE WAT WAS HELD in a brace of rigid vines: purple bougainvillea peeled old lime plaster in chunks shaped like continents. I peeked waist-high pockmarks among the flowers, the distinct signature of old gunfire, never repaired and slowly leeching puce from the straw-clay at the core of the bousillage walls. Without my being aware of learning the skill, my senses had become expert at finding traces of warfare. Pacing the plaza, my eyes drawn up by this intuitive force, I saw that the temple's bell in its tower was made of an emptied air-drop bomb. The bell was silent, and yet I sensed its presence rippling like sound through the air.

I added my shoes to the pile outside the wat and went in. Adjusting to the deeper tint of the indoors, I saw first the glimmer of a gilded Buddha sitting cross-legged on a dais. I discerned this through a thin grayness, as if the air was worn out. One of Buddha's hands was raised with thumb and middle finger hooked, a gesture to ward off evil; his other hand pointed to the ground to ask the earth to bear witness to suffering. Dirt crept across the floor and fled to the corners, where it collected in cloud-piles. Large wax castles loomed, fantasies of private hopes and dreams, now veiled with spidery dust and faded silk streamers. I looked up to see hanging origami birds folded from soda cans, glimmering ornaments. This was a place where the old was given new life or abandoned. Slashed and strung in garlands, plastic water bottles made elegant, translucent flowers: calyx and corolla unfurled from blue bottle caps.

Under Buddha's lowered gaze and Vanida's meticulous guidance, the village council was sketching the major landmarks: the road, the mountains, the temple, the school, village houses, shrines, and fields. Large butcher paper rolls and markers zigzagged over the tiled floor. Sitting before the dais, the village residents and the clearance team faced each other like adversaries in a debate. Representatives from each household sat on rush mats, bristling boredom. Vanida gestured me to a cushion near her on the side of the clearance team.

The village council was unfamiliar with cartographic symbols. Vanida patiently taught them that roofed rectangles stood for houses, parallel lines for roads, and arrows for compass directions, etc. An older councilwoman drew the school symbol sideways, finding the red belltower (a shape that reminded me of American pioneer schoolhouses) difficult to interpret.

During the war, I heard the chief tell the survey technicians, residents had scavenged landmines to protect the village border. They had removed most of the mines after the war but still found them once in a while. The location of the old minefield went on the map, too: a dashed red curve.

"There are no bombs around here," said an elder man on the village council.

"We don't have a lot of bombs," said a young woman holding two small children. "You should go somewhere else where they need more clearance."

"Why did they send you? We need clean water, not clearance!" said a woman hunched near the back. A grizzled man shouted his response, perhaps sparking a familiar antagonism between them, "Whoever comes, comes. We should be happy when *anyone* comes!"

The room grumbled, then hushed into pent displeasure. Smartphones lit up youngster's faces in the crowd.

"What about the bomb bell?" I asked the council, following my uncertainty through the stale air. "Where did that come from?"

"Oh, we bought that from our scrap trader," said the elder on the council, "It's from Vietnam."

Underground, I imagined them. A farmer plowing his field found nearly three hundred ancient Buddha figurines. Rumor said they were gold, but the photograph in the national news showed statuettes covered in black scrim—they must be bronze. Relics from the ancient kingdom of Lan Xang, a blessing for the young Lao state, the farmer said to the press. He donated them to the national museum in Vientiane (I know that there is a case in the museum filled with defused cluster submunitions, carefully cleaned and labeled, the museum staff curating what would otherwise destroy itself). The soil in Laos was unruly, turning history over on itself, like a sea that sometimes churns up ancient coins. The farmer might easily have dug up something else with his plow—and it was this something else that made the news story a blessing.

The war continued beneath our feet. In her risk education programs, Vanida taught people the most common ways that they might find, and set off, a bomb. Most of these involved digging. When tending their water buffalo, people often staked the animals, leashed, so that they could pasture in areas without fences. Hammering the stake into the ground was enough. Using a machete to cut bamboo shoots was enough. Digging for mushrooms or grubs or roots was enough. Plowing a field was enough. Using a farm tool to shore up terraces for a new rice planting was enough. Building the foundation for a house was enough. Setting a fire in a cook pit was enough. Vanida taught people to dig down the length of a hand to check for bombs in the earth before beginning their work.

Military waste changed my relationship to the ground and to time. The war was a layer underground that I might dig into by choice or accident. I sensed that there was another reality just beneath the surface where violence continued; these were the many layers of social life, some felt and some harder to feel. A society that normalized inequality taught us to misrecognize violence, to push it beneath and out of sight. I imagined it like walking on thin ice: a danger not easily seen from the shore. A brown hand tells above the surface of the broken ice, but we do not see it as a drowning plea for help.

Underground, the mouths of hungry ghosts opened and closed. Once, I saw a bomb cradled within the roots of a tree. The clearance team met to assess the risk: How likely was it to explode in the tree's roots? How much pressure does a tree root exert? How much would it cost in time and money to remove the tree in order to clear the bomb? Was removing the tree safer or riskier than just leaving the bomb where it was? How likely was a person to find the bomb if it was under a tree? Was it safe enough?

What is safe enough? I imagined Chantha's grandmother digging the family's dirt house.

My mind jumped again, and I remembered Vanida digging on a signal from her detector in that dry field on the cusp of the monsoon. She knelt, using her hands to gently scoop the soil behind her. Moving slowly, fingers dusted with fine grains, barely dirty. Careful, thoughtful digging into history—a kind of exorcism of a violent past. She touched the buried item as if through gloves, the white kind made of soft cotton that my grandmother wore dancing. I tried to feel the thin line of contact, the bare distance, between safety and danger.

When Vanida and I arrived for her scheduled risk training that evening, there was nobody at the wat.

Vanida circled the plaza, as if trying to gather women from under the banana leaves. Finally, completing her circuit and finding only me, she said: "We have to go get more women and children for the training. Let's split up: you go that way, I'll go this way."

Walking my assigned direction, I heard her voice behind me politely fussing the farmers in their vegetable patch: "Hello, we are having a women's meeting about bombs in a few minutes. Please come to the wat for the meeting."

"Oh, maybe later. We are busy with this eggplant," I heard one of the farmers push her off.

The women that I spoke to were all very polite, but each already had other more pressing plans. I was probably not the best representative and lacked Vanida's energy for the training. Many women were still working in the rice paddies, I was told by their husbands. Without my trying, I gathered a small crowd of chickens nosing my legs for scraps.

I met Vanida back sitting alone on the temple steps. While we had searched, night had descended and our faces were shadowed; we were merely the shapes of people without expressions.

Looking up, the milky way was visible a little above the horizon. I realized that the stars were all different colors, delicate shades of yellow, orange, and pink. Being born in a city, and unused to true night, I wondered at this starlight that was barely light, but seemed to gently suffuse objects with absence. Below, few houses had electricity, and the shadows of the houses were made into one impenetrable shape, thick and very crisp. There was a darker line of trees on the horizon, rising into a scalloped edge like lace on a tablecloth, beneath the bluer sky illuminated by the milky way. The deeper darkness was here on earth.

A sizzle caught my eye, and I noticed a young monk watching us from a temple window, smoking a cigarette. There was no other activity in the plaza.

"I wonder why, why he didn't tell anyone! Is it that he doesn't care? Is he just lazy? Or maybe he doesn't understand about the bombs?" she said in English. I heard her heavy sigh next to me. "I want to help people to have better lives. But sometimes I feel that we live in different worlds: he lives in the village and I live in the city. Their world is very small, and I want to show them that they can do different things. I want to educate them."

"I don't know why, Vanida." It was strange to talk to her without seeing her face. I hesitated to say more—my suspicions about the war scrap trader who sold the temple bomb bell; my concerns about hosting the clearance events at the Buddhist wat. Buddhism is the religion of the lowland cites and the state. I wondered if the monks were outsiders, settlers sent from the lowlands to convert animist villagers. I remembered the halfhearted audience at the village mapping.

"Most of the folks in the village practice spirit cults—maybe they think the clearance is a Buddhist project since all the events are at the temple?"

Her gloomy shape shrugged. "Maybe. But why is there a temple up here at all if the villagers don't go there?"

Women and children began to trickle into the plaza, some holding lanterns, and settle in a paltry crowd in front of the steps. The temple lights zapped on and immediately, as if waiting nearby, moths arrived floating like ashes in the breeze. It was now dark enough that I could not read the fieldnotes I was writing.

"What did you have for dinner and was it delicious?" Vanida, newly invigorated, began to talk to the crowd.

"It was delicious!" a few of the children chorused.

"Did you have rice?"

"Yes, we had rice!"

"Have you seen bombs in the ban?"

Nearly everyone raised their hands, and all of the adult women. Vanida took out a folder I knew was labeled Commonly Found Items and removed a sheaf of laminated photos. The photos were copied from American training manuals and still had the English names printed at the top. She held one up so that the photo was just visible under the fizzing temple lights.

"Have you seen this?" It was a BLU-3, bright yellow, but hard to see in the dim. Now she was speaking in a voice for children that was bright and inviting.

"Yes!"

"Where do you see it?"

"When gathering bamboo!" a small girl offered from the cradle of her mother's lap.

"Do you know what this is?"

Several little ones shouted: "It's a candle!"

I had seen in these upland houses cleaved cluster bomblets filled with oil and on fire with a far less dangerous heat. Even after Dao told me of her childhood growing up with bomb-candles, I was still shocked to hear children misidentifying bombs. Bombs became unremarkable for them, but not for me.

"No, it's a bomb." Vanida corrected the children. "Do you know what a bomb is?"

Silence. A boy guessed: "Sometimes they explode . . ."

"Yes, bombs explode and are dangerous. Ba-ba-ba-BOOM!" She advanced on her audience with the photo outstretched and spooked the children into fearful laughter. "We have a Lao word for this one. Do you know it?"

"It's called a bombie!"

"Yes, a bombie is a small bomb that can explode and kill you. What should you do if you find one?"

An older boy, with a forager's knife tied around his bare chest, replied in an even, practiced voice: "When you find a bomb, tell the chief, your father, or your teacher and leave it where it is."

"Perfect. Exactly. Did you hear that? When you find a bomb, don't touch it and tell an adult!"

She turned to the adults in the crowd. "Have any of you ever opened a bombie?"

Every woman's hand went up. Vanida singled out an older woman, clearly well-known, to the crowd's delight. "You have opened bombs."

"Yes," the woman gave Vanida an incredulous glance from her boots to her cap. A *so what, and who are you?* look.

"Do you think that bombs are scary?"

"Yes!" and she slapped her thighs, making the crowd laugh with her. "But I don't have fear when I open them, only after."

Chatter overtook parts of the crowd. A few women got up to leave. Vanida tried to draw back their interest with the story of a woman who was blinded by an explosion in this village last month. She described the accident: the woman hitting a bomb in a rice paddy. It exploded. Blood was coming out of her eyes like this— Vanida wriggled her hands down her face and body, mimicking the spray of blood. It had taken two hours to get her to the hospital, and now she was blind. The woman was resting at home, but unable to walk and thus wasn't at the training. Bombs are dangerous, do not touch them! It was a grisly tale, but it didn't capture the crowd in the way that Vanida had hoped. Old news.

She tried a second time to draw back their attention. Pointing to the professed bomb-opener, she declared that the woman had to sing a song about bombs or nominate another woman to sing a song. The woman nominated another so quickly that the second was pulled up to the porch with only one shoe. The crowd burst into harsh laughter. The song Vanida and the woman made up went like this:

Bombs are dangerous! Ah!
Bombs are dangerous in our yard!
Bombs are dangerous in our field!
Bombs are dangerous in our school!
Bombs are dangerous! Boom-boom!

Vanida and the woman jumped in a circle with their knees high. Their distended shadows jumped beneath them. An onlooker threw the second shoe up the steps—it missed the woman but made her jump higher. Children in the crowd cruelly drove on the dancers.

The sight of their elongated, skeletal shadows brought to my mind, unbidden, Huynh Cong Ut's familiar black-and-white photograph of napalmed, howling children holding their scorched arms out like wings, the horizon billowing fire behind them. The two images hovered before me: the gray light, the distorted faces of the children, a similarity in the open arc of their arms, a sense of being lifted out of the everyday as birds in flight are lifted by heated air. From the first, photographs required an explosion, not least in war photography—flash powders were similar to gunpowder, and many early photographers injured themselves in the flash of the shot. For Huynh's war photographs, explosives were no longer a technical requirement, but the subject of the photograph. And then came to my mind a song I learned from a retired American Air Force officer who had worked defoliation operations in Vietnam and Laos. That song went like this:

> We shoot the sick, the young, the lame
> We do our best to kill and maim
> Because the kills all count the same
> Napalm sticks to kids!
>
> Eighteen kids in a no-fire zone
> Books on their arms as they go home
> The last in line goes home alone
> Napalm sticks to kids!

The performance appeared to be the end of the women's attention, and many began to leave. Mothers relit their lanterns and, taking their children in hand, disappeared back into their dark houses. Vanida, exhausted, let them go. Above us, controlled by some unknown source, the temple light zapped back out. Vanida and I gathered our supplies, including the Commonly Found Items folder, in the dark.

"Come on, there's one last thing..."

Without a lantern of our own, we walked like somnambulists without sight through our memories of the village. At the end of the path, the chief's house was tall on stilts and accessed by a long ladder. By feel, we took our shoes off, climbed up the ladder, and limbered ourselves into the single square room. The walls were windowless, and the sole light came from a bulb swinging from the roof timber. A young woman rocked a baby in a hammock—I did not recognize her from the training. The family watched a tiny television on a table, the only piece of furniture.

"Hello, we are the local clearance team! You have a beautiful ban. Very nice. We are here because we need your stamp on our documents for the risk education training."

The old man stared at her, and I thought perhaps he didn't speak Lao. Then he turned and rummaged in the back of the room, behind a bamboo partition. He emerged with a small plastic bag. The man slowly untwisted the bag and drew out a tin of ink and a wooden-handled stamp. Vanida pointed out to him where he needed to stamp, and he did so without the slightest hesitation. Perfunctory, bureaucratic, and without speaking a word. And then we cautiously scooted ourselves out and down the stairs. The ladder swung unsteadily, and Vanida nearly slipped on the thin rungs—I remembered that she had said she was from another world.

That was the chief who had failed to inform the villagers about the women's meeting. Walking back beneath the glitterdark dome of the milky way, Vanida sighed with frustration: "I've never had this much trouble with a village."

In a field of stumps, where shorn trees tangled like twine, and the soil was scalped of grasses, the blue tags of the clearance markers were easy for me to sight.

Syha and Channarong, who was fighting off a cold, bent nose to sniffling nose over a dig. Syha had one leg in the hole and was reaching down to pry open what looked, at first, like a dirty beer cooler. Revealed inside the case, metal cylinders were stacked neat as packs of Budweiser. Channarong looked up: he was flushed but happy, red-nosed.

"It's incredible!"

"Okay, show me why I should be excited about this."

I worked my way to the edge of the pit. The fresh soil was spidered with hacked roots and sniffed of sweet cut wood. Patches of white paint were still visible on the case, now dirty except for the black stenciled label that had mysteriously kept its freshness while interred. I read the label: ADAPTER CLUSTER BOMB ADU 253/B. In Syha's hands, the top hinge swung smoothly even though two of the case's corners were split like a crumpled paper box. Tree roots had forced their way into the seams, perhaps seeking mineral ichor.

"It's mind-boggling: fifty years after war and we're still finding new kinds of bombs!" Channarong hopped over to my side of the pit, pointing at his find. "It's a totally new kind of dispenser: it's payload would have been seventy-seven BLU-3/Bs, and we think these cases came in packs of twenty-four, so the total load was something like 5,544 bombs. Very big payloads and even bigger strike patterns!"

Syha, less excited: "We have never considered what the size of such a strike would be on the ground and how much survey we would have to do."

Channarong nodded but was impervious to Syha's solemn tone. "We're training our team leaders so they understand how difficult it can be to assess the edges of a strike. We've been finding some very big strikes in this area. When we find a bomb at the predicted edge of a strike, we clear an extra ten-meter diameter from the border, just to make sure we've cleared the whole strike. This is called a fade out. But with these massive strikes, we keep finding more and more bombs at the border, and the edge keeps fading out. No one else that I know of has found a dispenser this big, and this helps explain the size of the strikes. We can't assume anything in these old secret battlefields."

He pointed at the black lettering. "This nomenclature . . . we wouldn't be able to recognize this thing, except your American ancestors nicely wrote the specs on the side. There's no record of these being used in Laos, probably top secret, but I found design records of a similar ADU 253, and I'm basing my predictions on that. Do you want to touch the case? Totally safe, I promise."

I hesitated for a moment, then knelt on my heels to reach into the pit. Bits of crag and dirt jittered off the case when I made contact. The metal was warming, losing its underground chill now that it was exposed to the daylight. I retracted my hand, suddenly uncomfortable, as if I had touched the cooling corpse of a relative. I felt the presence of my kin, the pilots and bombers who flew the Pacific. The American bombings turned the land into a murderous reliquary. In America, we bury our dead: to bury, to put to rest. But here in Laos, where the dead are cremated and not buried, our errors are not redeemed by their internment in the earth. There is no rest in these graves. Things buried endure. When I startled, Syha reached out prepared to catch me before I fell into the pit. We made private eye-contact, and I shook my head, no, it's fine, I'm not going to fall.

"So . . . are you going to name it after yourself?"

Grinning at me, Channarong tipped his hat and then sneezed. "I'm going to name it after my daughter."

"Do you name all your favorite bombs after children? Your daughter's name is Noi, which means *small* but this is a very big bomb. Noi nyai labaerd, *little big bomb*?"

Syha, quite understandably, had not a stitch of humor: "It is bad luck to name a bomb after a child."

"How big would a strike be for this dispenser?" I asked Channarong.

"We actually don't know," he sobered a bit. "If anyone tells you that they can recognize a strike pattern, they are lying. It is just too uncertain, even with all the data in the world. Think about it: we're trying to predict footprints based on strikes from forty, fifty years ago. In any given area, it is not just one strike. You might have one plane going this direction, one plane going that direction. It is impossible to pick out which bombs come from which planes based on the evidence. It is never a clear, simple egg pattern; it is layers of ellipses. But something like this . . . ?"

With a hand that almost shook, he pointed to the case in its pit, exhumed after fifty years. He radiated an incongruous ruddy excitement.

"Something like this?" he repeated, "This is the find I was hoping to make because it explains some really massive strikes that go on forever. It is very difficult to find the edges. We don't know where it ends."

Acknowledgments

I dedicate this book to my Aunt Robyn: I cherished reading my writing out loud to you, fully warmed by your appetite for my work, regardless of genre. You brought the same excitement to my "new novel" that you brought to your summer mystery reads—I am privileged to have had one such reader in my life and will be lucky to find another. I wish with all my heart that you had read this book; I do not believe in heaven, but I know that you do.

I wish to acknowledge the support of Marcela Maxfield, my editor at Stanford University Press, and Sunna Juhn, her editorial assistant. Marcela brought the dedication and flexibility necessary to bring this hybrid project to press. My Laos research required more imagination than I have previously brought to my ethnographies, and I am grateful to have an editor who shared my vision of creative scholarship. This book would not exist without her insightful readings and editorial guidance.

I wish to thank Tisse Takagi, my agent, for her support of my scholarly and literary work. The writing is easier knowing that I am not doing this alone. I am privileged to have the backing of Tisse and the other agents and staff of The Science Factory.

ACKNOWLEDGMENTS

I am grateful to the people who shared their stories with me during my Lao fieldwork. I wrote this book to honor them, while still
protecting their identities. I hope that they recognize their strengths
and challenges in my stories.

Finally, I am grateful for the support of the members of my writing circle: Kimberley McKinson and Deborah Jones. They were
the first to read my drafts for Strike Patterns, and their good advice
is indelibly stamped in these pages. We three are writing our books
together: here is mine, and I look forward to seeing two more books
published in the future.

Further Reading

To aid the reader, and in lieu of a bibliography, I include a collection of books and articles on Laos, cluster bombing, and ethnographic fiction. This list preferences works written for the public and readily accessible from the municipal or university library.

LAOS

Evans, Grant. 2003. *A Short History of Laos: The Land in Between.* Revised Edition. Crows Nest, NSW: Allen & Unwin.

Stuart-Fox, Martin. 1997. *A History of Laos.* Cambridge: Cambridge University Press.

Bouté, Vanina and Vatthana Pholsena, editors. 2017. *Changing Lives in Laos: Society, Politics, and Culture in a Post-Socialist State.* Singapore: National University of Singapore Press.

THE SECRET WAR

Branfman, Fred, editor. 2013 (1972). *Voices from the Plain of Jars: Life Under an Air War.* Second Edition. Madison: University of Wisconsin Press.

Convention on Cluster Munitions. 2008. United Nations Development Program, Dublin, May 30. http://www.clusterconvention.org.

Jacobs, Seth. 2012. *The Universe Unraveling: American Foreign Policy in Cold War Laos.* Ithaca, NY: Cornell University Press.

LCMM. 2019. "Lao PDR: Mine Ban Policy." *The Landmine & Cluster Munition Monitor.* http://www.the-monitor.org/en-gb/reports/2019/lao-pdr/mine-ban-policy.aspx

Kurlantzick, Joshua. 2017. *A Great Place to Have a War: America in Laos and the Birth of a Military CIA.* New York: Simon and Schuster.

Morrison, Gayle L. 1999. *Sky Is Falling: An Oral History of the CIA's Evacuation of the Hmong from Laos.* Jefferson, NC: McFarland & Company.

Prokosch, Eric. 1995. *The Technology of Killing: A Military and Political History of Antipersonnel Weapons.* London: Zed Books.

Yang, Kao Kalia. 2017. *The Latehomecomer: A Hmong Family Memoir.* Minneapolis, MN: Coffee House Press.

Zani, Leah. 2019. *Bomb Children: Life in the Former Battlefields of Laos.* Durham, NC: Duke University Press.

WRITING AGAINST TERROR

Nordstrom, Carolyn. 1997. *A Different Kind of War Story.* Philadelphia: University of Pennsylvania Press.

Sluka, Jeffrey A. editor. 2000. *Death Squad: The Anthropology of State Terror.* Philadelphia: University of Pennsylvania Press.

Tuassig, Michael T. 1987. *Shamanism, Colonialism, and the Wild Man: A Study in Terror and Healing.* Chicago: University of Chicago Press.

ETHNOGRAPHIC FICTION

Geertz, Clifford. 1988. *Works and Lives: The Anthropologist as Author.* Stanford, CA: Stanford University Press.

Ghosh, Amitav. 1993. *In an Antique Land: History in the Guise of a Traveler's Tale.* New York: A. A. Knopf.

Hurston, Zora Neale. 2008 (1935). *Mules and Men.* New York: Harper Perennial Modern Classics.

Hurston, Zora Neale. 2006 (1937). *Their Eyes Were Watching God: 75th Anniversary Edition.* New York: Amistad.

Latour, Bruno. 1996. *Aramis, or The Love of Technology.* Cambridge, MA: Harvard University Press.

Le Guin, Ursula K. 2000 (1969). *The Left Hand of Darkness: 50th Anniversary Edition.* New York: Ace Science Fiction.

Lévi-Strauss, Claude. 2012 (1955). *Tristes Tropiques*. New York: Penguin Classics.

McGranahan, Carole. 2015. "Genre-Bending, or the Love of Ethnographic Fiction." *Savage Minds*. April 13, 2015. https://savageminds. org/2015/04/13/genre-bending-or-the-love-of-ethnographic-fiction/

McLean, Stuart. 2017. *Fictionalizing Anthropology*. Minneapolis: University of Minnesota Press.

McLean, Stuart and Anand Pandian, editors. 2017. *Crumpled Paper Boat: Experiments in Ethnographic Writing*. Durham, NC: Duke University Press.

Pandian, Anand. 2019. *A Possible Anthropology: Methods for Uneasy Times*. Durham, NC: Duke University Press.

Tarde, Gabriel. 1905. *Underground Man*. London: Duckworth & Co.

Raffles, Hugh. 2020. *The Book of Uncomformities: Speculations on Lost Time*. New York: Pantheon.

Stewart, Kathleen. 2007. *Ordinary Affects*. Durham, NC: Duke University Press.

Visweswaran, Kamala. 1994. *Fictions of Feminist Ethnography*. Minneapolis: University of Minnesota Press.